I0436654

Creating NPM Package with ReactJS

React JavaScript Guide to Create, Test, and Publish NPM Libraries

CodeSweetly

Creating NPM Package with ReactJS

React JavaScript Guide to Create, Test, and Publish NPM Libraries

© 2024 – 2026 Oluwatobi Sofela

All rights reserved.

No part of this publication may be reproduced, stored in a retrieval system, or transmitted in any form or by any means, electronic, mechanical, photocopying, recording, or otherwise, without express written permission of the publisher. It is illegal to copy this book, post it to a website, or distribute it by any other means without permission, except for the use of brief quotations in a book review.

This book is provided "as is" and "as available" without any warranty. While the author has taken every precaution to ensure the accuracy of this book's information, in no event shall the author, company, or publisher be liable in whatsoever way for any loss or damages, including but not limited to any consequential, indirect, special, or incidental damages caused or alleged to be caused directly or indirectly by this book's content.

The names, contact information, characters, and incidents portrayed in this book are the work of the author's imagination. Any resemblance to actual persons, events or localities is entirely coincidental.

First published in 2024

Revised and updated edition published in 2026

www.codesweetly.com

Tweet This Book!

Please help CodeSweetly by spreading the word about this book on Twitter!

The suggested hashtag for this book is #reactjs.

Find out what other people are saying about the book by clicking on this link to search for this hashtag on Twitter:

#reactjs

Also By CodeSweetly

Learn Coding Visually
Code React Sweetly
Creating NPM Package with TypeScript
Creating NPM Package with Vanilla JavaScript
Creating NPM Package with React TypeScript
The CSS Grid Guidebook
Visual CSS Grid
Visual CSS Flexbox
CSS Flexbox

Contents

CONTENTS

Introduction

Welcome to the World of NPM Packages!

NPM (Node Package Manager) is a vast database ecosystem that hosts thousands of reusable code packages. Developers use it to share, manage, discover, and install libraries that solve everyday problems or add functionality to their applications.

 Packages are sometimes called libraries, plugins, frameworks, or tools. It is simply a directory (or project) that includes a `package.json` file for recording key information about the package.

Publishing your own NPM package is an empowering way to contribute to the developer community, grow your skills, and build a portfolio-worthy product. In doing so, you will strengthen a range of valuable abilities, including:

- Communication
- Collaboration
- Organization
- Problem-solving
- Documentation
- Technical development

Becoming a package publisher allows you to take your ideas from concept to a distributable product that others can integrate into their projects. It is a great way to stand out as a developer.

This book is a practical guide to creating, testing, and publishing your own NPM packages using ReactJS. No prior publishing experience is required.

Why This Book Will Help You

Learning to publish NPM packages is not a craft you master by merely reading or watching tutorials—it is a skill you develop by doing.

That is why this book is project-based and hands-on. Along the way, you will build a working NPM package while applying new concepts immediately in a real-world scenario.

To get the most out of this book, open your code editor (like VS Code) and follow along with the examples. Doing so will keep you from falling into "tutorial hell"—where you watch countless tutorials but never actually build anything.

What You Will Build

You will develop a functional and customizable Tweet Button package throughout the book.

While this library might sound simple, don't underestimate it. This project is designed to teach you the essential skills and patterns required to publish any NPM package. Once you understand the process, you will have the ability to scale your own ideas to any level of complexity.

Use the Right Tools

To ensure smooth progress, it is best to use the exact versions of dependencies listed in this book. This helps avoid unexpected issues that might arise from newer versions.

After completing the project, feel free to upgrade the dependencies. If anything breaks, check online documentation or community discussions for solutions.

What You Should Know First

Knowing the basics of Git, GitHub, React, and JavaScript will make it easier to learn how to publish NPM packages. It's helpful to be familiar with these tools before you start.

Got Questions?

If you have questions or comments about this book, email con-tact@codesweetly.com or send me a direct message on Twitter (@oluwatobiss).

Let's Get Started!

The next chapter will show you how to set up the project.

Project Configuration

Below is the required system and file configurations for creating NPM packages.

1. Set Up Your System

Ensure your system has the following installations:

- Git
- Node 22.13 (or greater)
- NPM 10.9 (or greater)

- Refer to the Git tutorial[1] to install, update, or verify Git on your system.
- See the package manager[2] tutorial for steps to install, update, or verify Node and NPM.

2. Create a Project Directory

Create a new folder for your project as follows:

Figure 1. Command Line

```
1   mkdir thank-you-tweet-button-001
```

You may use any name. For example, this tutorial uses `thank-you-tweet-button-001`.

[1]https://codesweetly.com/how-to-use-git#how-to-use-git
[2]https://codesweetly.com/package-manager-explained

- Choose a name[3] with 214 characters or fewer.
- Use only lowercase letters in your project name.
- Do not include "js" or "node" in your package name.

Afterward, navigate to your project directory using the command line:

Figure 2. The Syntax to Change to a Different Directory
```
1   cd path/to/thank-you-tweet-button-001
```

3. Create a package.json File

Use NPM to initialize a package.json file[4] for your project.

Figure 3. Command Line
```
1   npm init -y
```

4. Configure the Project as an ES Module NPM Package

This guide uses ES Modules in all JavaScript files, so add a `"type": "module"` field to your project's `package.json` file.

Figure 4. package.json: Set up package as an ES Module library (line 5)
```
1   {
2     "scripts": {
3       "test": "echo \"Error: no test specified\" && exit 1"
4     },
5     "type": "module"
6   }
```

You should also initialize Git at this stage.

5. Initialize a Git Repository

Create a `.git` repo in your project's root directory[5]:

---

[3]https://docs.npmjs.com/cli/v8/configuring-npm/package-json#name
[4]https://codesweetly.com/package-json-file-explained
[5]https://codesweetly.com/web-tech-terms-r#root-directory

Figure 5. Command Line

```
1    git init
```

6. Specify the Files Git Should Ignore

Create a `.gitignore` file in your project's root directory:

Figure 6. Command Line

```
1    touch .gitignore
```

Afterward, open the newly created `.gitignore` file[6] and write the names of the files, folders, or file types you want Git to ignore.

Here's an example:

Figure 7. .gitignore

```
1    /node_modules
2    /dist
```

The snippet above instructs Git to ignore tracking the current directory's `node_modules` and `dist` folders.

- A current directory is the folder in which you are currently working.
- A current directory is sometimes called a "current working directory (CWD)" or "working directory."

Now, stage and commit your recent changes.

7. Stage and Commit Your Project's Changes to Git

Run the following command in your terminal to stage and commit your recent changes.

---

[6]https://codesweetly.com/how-to-use-git/#example-of-a-gitignore-file

Figure 8. Command Line

```
1   git add -A && git commit -m "Initialize project using CodeSweetly's guide"
```

The command above tells Git to stage and commit all modified and untracked files in the project.

Next, configure a remote repository for the project.

8. Configure a GitHub Remote Repository

1. Go to the GitHub website[7] and sign in or create an account[8] if you do not have one.
2. After signing in, create a new GitHub repository. You may use `thank-you-tweet-button-001` or another name of your choice.
3. Once you've created a remote repository for your package, link your project's `.git` directory (located locally on your system) with the remote repository on GitHub. To connect to the remote repository, go to your package's root directory via your local terminal and run the `git remote add` command. Here's the syntax:

Figure 9. Command Line

```
1   git remote add origin https://github.com/your-username/remote-repo-name.git
```

- Replace `your-username` in the code above with your GitHub username. Likewise, replace `remote-repo-name` with your remote repository's name.
- See GitHub Docs[9] to learn more on creating a GitHub repository.

You can also add the remote repo to your `package.json` file for easy access to people who want to contribute to your project.

---

[7]https://github.com
[8]https://github.com/signup
[9]https://docs.github.com/en/github/getting-started-with-github/create-a-repo

Figure 10. package.json: Add repository field (line 4-7)

```
1  {
2    "name": "thank-you-tweet-button-001",
3    "version": "1.0.0",
4    "repository": {
5      "type": "git",
6      "url": "https://github.com/your-username/app-repo-name.git"
7    },
8    "scripts": {
9      "test": "echo \"Error: no test specified\" && exit 1"
10   }
11 }
```

Let's provide the remote repo's issues URL as the package's bug tracker. And an email people can use to report issues:

Figure 11. package.json: Add bugs field (line 8-11)

```
1  {
2    "name": "thank-you-tweet-button-001",
3    "version": "1.0.0",
4    "repository": {
5      "type": "git",
6      "url": "https://github.com/your-username/app-repo-name.git"
7    },
8    "bugs": {
9      "url": "https://github.com/your-username/app-repo-name/issues",
10     "email": "your-project-email@host.com"
11   },
12   "scripts": {
13     "test": "echo \"Error: no test specified\" && exit 1"
14   }
15 }
```

Afterward, stage and commit your changes:

Figure 12. Command Line

```
1  git add -A && git commit -m "Create repository and bugs fields"
```

Next, push your local Git repository to the remote repository.

9. Push Your Local Git Directory to the Remote Repo

After successfully connecting your local directory to the remote repository, you can begin pushing (uploading) your local project to the remote repository. Here's how:

Figure 13. Command Line

```
1   git push -u origin main
```

The command above instructs Git to push your local `main` branch's `.git` directory to the remote `origin` branch on GitHub.

 If you refresh the main page of your remote repository, you should see your upload.

Now it's time to set up your project with React.

10. Install React

Install React as a development dependency

Figure 14. Command Line

```
1   npm i -D react@19.2.4
```

The command above tells NPM to install `react` as your package's development dependency.

- The `react` package is a library containing React's core functionality for creating React components.
- `i` is the shorthand notation for `install`.
- The `-D` flag is the shorthand notation for `--save-dev`.

You may wonder why React is installed as a development dependency if users need it in production. The following explains the reasoning.

Why Install React as a Package's Dev-Dependency?

Installing React as a development dependency prevents users from being required to download React when installing your package.

React requires only one copy of the `react` package per project. Therefore, specifying React as a dev-dependency prevents users from having to download React when installing your package. If their project already has a React copy, they wouldn't need to install another one.

One thing to note: your package will only work in projects that already have React installed. But there's a good workaround:

- Duplicate the `"react"` property from your package.json `"devDependencies"` field into the `"peerDependencies"` field as shown:

Figure 15. package.json: Add peerDependencies field (line 5-7)

```
1  {
2    "devDependencies": {
3      "react": "^19.2.4"
4    },
5    "peerDependencies": {
6      "react": "^19.2.4"
7    }
8  }
```

Specifying React as a peer-dependency tells package managers to check whether the app installing your package contains the listed `peerDependencies`. If so, the application has the dependencies your package needs to work.

If the package manager cannot find the `peerDependencies`, some NPM versions (such as 7 and 11) will install them automatically. Other versions (such as 3-6) will display a warning that informs the user to install the dependencies manually.

dependencies vs. devDependencies vs. peerDependencies

- `"dependencies"` specify the packages a project depends on in production (when your app is running on a live server).

- The "devDependencies" field lists all the packages a project does not need in production, but requires for its local development and testing purposes.
- "peerDependencies" list all the packages a project expects its host application to have in its node_modules directory.

Stage and commit your changes:

Figure 16. Command Line

```
1   git add -A && git commit -m "Install react"
```

After configuring the project, continue to the next chapter to learn how to write a test case for your component.

Testing React Component

Here are the steps to write a test case for your component.

1. Install the Testing Tools

First, install the test packages your project needs:

Figure 17. Command Line

```
1  npm i -D vitest@4.1.5 @testing-library/react@16.3.2
```

- `vitest` is a test runner that runs your test scripts and displays test results in the command line.
- `@testing-library/react` is the React Testing Library. It provides the APIs you need to write test cases for your React components.

2. Specify Vitest as Your Project's Test Runner Tool

Update your package's `test` script to use Vitest as the test runner.

Figure 18. package.json: Update test field (line 5)

```
1  {
2    "name": "thank-you-tweet-button-001",
3    "version": "1.0.0",
4    "scripts": {
5      "test": "vitest run"
6    }
7  }
```

3. Create Your Code Files

Create the following files in the root directory of your project.

- `index.js`: Entry point for the package.
- `TweetButton.jsx`: Codebase for the Tweet button component.
- `TweetButton.test.jsx`: Test file for the Tweet button component.

Figure 19. Command Line

```
1   touch index.js TweetButton.jsx TweetButton.test.jsx
```

4. Write Your Test Case

Since the goal is to create a Tweet button NPM package, it's important to test that your Tweet button component renders correctly. Open the new test file (`TweetButton.test.jsx`) and add the following test case:

Figure 20. TweetButton.test.jsx

```
1   import { test } from "vitest";
2   import { render } from "@testing-library/react";
3   import { TweetButton } from "./TweetButton";
4
5   test("tweet button renders correctly", () => {
6     render(<TweetButton />);
7   });
```

Here's what the test snippet above does:

- It imports the packages you need to write the test case.
- It includes a test that checks if the `<TweetButton />` component renders without errors.

If you run the test now, it will fail because the component hasn't been built yet. Let's build it next.

5. Develop Your React Component

Open your `TweetButton.jsx` file and build the Tweet button component so it passes the test:

Figure 21. TweetButton.jsx

```
1  export function TweetButton() {
2    const tweetURL =
3      "https://twitter.com/intent/tweet?text=Thank+you,+%40oluwatobiss.+Your+bo⌐
   ↪   ok+helped+me+create,+test,+and+publish+an+NPM+package.%0A%0ACreating%⌐
   ↪   20NPM%20Package%0A%0Ahttps%3A%2F%2Famzn.to/4lifL3n";
4
5    return (
6      <div>
7        <a href={tweetURL} target="_blank">
8          Send a thank you tweet
9        </a>
10     </div>
11   );
12 }
```

- We used named exports[1] for the `TweetButton` component because default exports can be error-prone[2]. Package authors should use named exports when possible.
- Learn about default export[3].

6. Configure the Entry File

Use the entry file (`index.js`) to aggregate the assets you want users to import and use in their apps.

Figure 22. index.js

```
1  export { TweetButton } from "./TweetButton";
```

---

[1]https://codesweetly.com/javascript-modules-tutorial#how-to-export-a-modules-code
[2]https://esbuild.github.io/content-types/#default-interop
[3]https://codesweetly.com/javascript-modules-tutorial#how-to-export-anonymously-to-an-es-module

The component re-export statement[4] defines the package's public API, which users can import as shown below:

Figure 23. Example of how users can import your NPM package's public APIs into their application.

```
1  import { TweetButton } from "./your-package-name";
```

7. Install the Code Compiler

Vitest does not recognize JSX syntax by default. You need a compiler or build tools, such as Babel or Vite, to transform JSX into plain JavaScript. In this guide, we use Vite because of its seamless integration with Vitest.

Figure 24. Command Line

```
1  npm i -D vite@8.0.9 @vitejs/plugin-react@6.0.1
```

The above command installs `vite` and `@vitejs/plugin-react`.

- `vite`: the NPM distribution of Vite's core build tool, providing Vite's core development server, build system, and plugin infrastructure used to develop and bundle modern JavaScript applications.
- `@vitejs/plugin-react`: a Vite plugin that adds React support to Vite by enabling React Fast Refresh for seamless hot updates, configuring the Automatic JSX Runtime, and providing a Babel bridge for custom React transformations.

Now, let's configure Vite.

8. Configure Vite to Compile Your Code

Create a `vite.config.js` file in your project's root directory.

---

[4]https://codesweetly.com/javascript-modules-tutorial/#what-exactly-is-an-aggregator-file

Figure 25. Command Line

```
1   touch vite.config.js
```

Then, add the following configuration to the new file:

Figure 26. vite.config.js

```
1   import react from "@vitejs/plugin-react";
2   import { defineConfig } from "vite";
3   import { resolve } from "path";
4   import { readFileSync } from "fs";
5
6   const pkg = JSON.parse(
7     readFileSync(new URL("./package.json", import.meta.url), "utf8"),
8   );
9   const peerDependenciesNames = Object.keys(pkg.peerDependencies || {});
10
11  export default defineConfig({
12    plugins: [react()],
13    build: {
14      lib: {
15        entry: resolve(import.meta.dirname, "index.js"),
16        formats: ["es", "cjs"],
17        fileName: "index",
18      },
19      rolldownOptions: {
20        external: (moduleSpecifier) => {
21          return peerDependenciesNames.some(
22            (name) =>
23              moduleSpecifier === name || moduleSpecifier.startsWith(`${name}/`),
24          );
25        },
26      },
27    },
28  });
```

The configuration above instructs Vite to use the `react` plugin to transform your code into browser-compatible JavaScript.

- pkg: a variable containing the content of the project's `package.json` file.
- peerDependenciesNames: an array containing the names of `peerDepen-dencies` in the project's `package.json` file.
- defineConfig: a Vite helper that provides type hints, improves IDE autocompletion, and ensures the configuration is valid.

- `react`: a Vite plugin that adds support for React Fast Refresh, Automatic JSX Runtime, and custom React transformations.
- `build`: configures how Vite should compile the NPM Package's build output.
- `build.lib`: activates Vite's library mode.
- `build.lib.entry`: specifies the build-time entry module or modules that Vite uses as the starting point for building your project as a library.
- `build.lib.format`: the compilation formats you want to generate.
- `build.lib.fileName`: the name you want to use for the build output file. Vite will automatically append `.js` for ESM and `.cjs` for CommonJS.
- `rolldownOptions`: specifies Rolldown's build settings. (Note: Vite uses Rolldown internally to build libraries.)
- `rolldownOptions.external`: a list of runtime dependencies that you do not want Rolldown to include in your library's bundle.

 The function assigned to `rolldownOptions.external` checks whether an import statement's module specifier matches any library in the `peerDependenciesNames` array or one of its sub-paths, such as `"react"` or `"react/jsx-runtime"`. If a match is found, Rolldown marks the module as external, requiring the consuming application to provide the dependency.

9. Configure Vitest's Testing Environment

Vitest uses Node.js as its default testing environment. But since you're creating an NPM package for the web, you need a browser-like environment. Install the `jsdom` library:

Figure 27. Command Line

```
1  npm i -D jsdom@29.0.2
```

Next, add a `test` option to your `vite.config.js` file.

Figure 28. vite.config.js: Add test option (line 28-31)

```
1   import react from "@vitejs/plugin-react";
2   import { defineConfig } from "vite";
3   import { resolve } from "path";
4   import { readFileSync } from "fs";
5
6   const pkg = JSON.parse(
7     readFileSync(new URL("./package.json", import.meta.url), "utf8"),
8   );
9   const peerDependenciesNames = Object.keys(pkg.peerDependencies || {});
10
11  export default defineConfig({
12    plugins: [react()],
13    build: {
14      lib: {
15        entry: resolve(import.meta.dirname, "index.js"),
16        formats: ["es", "cjs"],
17        fileName: "index",
18      },
19      rolldownOptions: {
20        external: (moduleSpecifier) => {
21          return peerDependenciesNames.some(
22            (name) =>
23              moduleSpecifier === name || moduleSpecifier.startsWith(`${name}/`),
24          );
25        },
26      },
27    },
28    test: {
29      environment: "jsdom",
30      globals: false,
31    },
32  });
```

- `test.environment`: tells Vitest to use the `jsdom` test environment.
- `test.globals`: the `false` value prevents Vitest from globally injecting testing APIs like `describe`, `test`, and `expect`. This means you must explicitly import them in each test file. (Note: Many NPM Package authors prefer explicit imports because they improve clarity, editor support, avoid hidden globals, and make switching to other testing tools, like Jest, easier.)

10. Run the Test

Run the test to see if your program passes or fails.

Figure 29. Command Line

```
1   npm run test TweetButton.test.jsx
```

When you run the test, Vitest will show a pass or fail message in your editor's console. It looks like this:

Figure 30. Command Line

```
1   $ npm run test TweetButton.test.jsx
2
3   > thank-you-tweet-button-001@1.0.0 test
4   > vitest run TweetButton.test.jsx
5
6
7    RUN  v4.1.5 C:/Users/User/Documents/thank-you-tweet-button-001
8
9   ✓ TweetButton.test.jsx (1 test) 21ms
10     ✓ tweet button renders correctly 20ms
11
12  Test Files  1 passed (1)
13       Tests  1 passed (1)
14    Start at  01:31:16
15    Duration  7.12s (transform 62ms, setup 0ms, import 385ms, tests 21ms,
    ↪  environment 6.48s)
```

After you confirm your component works, stage and commit your changes:

Figure 31. Command Line

```
1   git add -A && git commit -m "Create Tweet button component"
```

Then push your commits to the remote repository:

Figure 32. Command Line

```
1   git push -u origin main
```

Up to now, you've used a basic format for commit messages. It's better to follow the Conventional Commits standard[5]. Let's look at that next.

 Note: Make sure you've committed and pushed your changes to GitHub before moving on to the next chapter.

---

[5]https://www.conventionalcommits.org

Commit Message Configuration

Conventional Commits is a standard way to write commit messages so both people and tools can easily understand them.

Conventional Commits Message Syntax

Below is the syntax you should use for writing a Conventional Commit message:

Figure 33. The Syntax of a Conventional Commit Message

```
1  type(scope): summary
```

- `type` is a noun, such as fix, feat, or chore, that specifies the nature of the changes being committed.
- `scope` is optional and indicates the package or file affected by the change. If used, enclose it in parentheses.
- A terminal colon (`:`) and space end the `type` and `scope` specification.
- `summary` is a short description of the commit.
- The `type`, `scope`, and `summary` together form the commit message header[1].

The 11 commit "type" developers often use

- `build`: for commits that affect the build process or external dependencies, such as updating an NPM package.
- `chore`: for commits that include maintenance tasks, such as updating the `.gitignore` file or an API key.
- `ci`: for commits that modify your CI (continuous integration)[2] configurations.
- `docs`: for commits that modify your project's documentation.

---

[1]https://codesweetly.com/how-to-use-git#what-are-the-three-main-parts-of-a-git-commit-message

- `feat`: for commits that introduce a new feature. This type corresponds to a MINOR release in Semantic Versioning (SemVer)[3].
- `fix`: for commits that resolve bugs. This type corresponds to a PATCH release in Semantic Versioning (SemVer).
- `perf`: for commits that improve your app's performance.
- `refactor`: for commits that restructure code, such as renaming a function.
- `revert`: for commits that return the codebase to a previous state. You may include the commit SHAs being reverted in the footer, for example: Refs: 7b804hrw, b394c306.
- `style`: for commits that adjust code formatting, such as adding semi-colons, whitespace, or indentation.
- `test`: for commits that modify your app's test code.

Many developers use plugins to make sure their commit messages follow the Conventional Commits format. This keeps messages consistent. Let's set up the same kind of checks in our workflow.

Enforcing the Conventional Commits Format

Install the `@commitlint/config-conventional` and `@commitlint/cli` packages to enforce the Conventional Commits format for your project's commit messages.

Figure 34. Command Line

```
1   npm i -D @commitlint/config-conventional@20.5.0 @commitlint/cli@20.5.0
```

The command above installs both `@commitlint/config-conventional` and `@commitlint/cli`.

- The `@commitlint/config-conventional` package provides configurable linting rules for commit messages. By default, it uses the Conventional Commits specification, but you can override these defaults with custom rules.

---

[2]https://en.wikipedia.org/wiki/CI/CD
[3]https://semver.org

- The @commitlint/cli package checks commit messages in the command-line interface using the conventions set in your project's commitlint.config.ts file.

After installing @commitlint/config-conventional, you still need to tell commitlint to use it. To do this, create a commitlint.config.js file in your project's root folder.

Figure 35. Command Line

```
1   touch commitlint.config.js
```

Then, add the following configuration to the newly created file:

Figure 36. commitlint.config.js

```
1   const Configuration = {
2     extends: ["@commitlint/config-conventional"],
3   };
4
5   export default Configuration;
```

The configuration above tells commitlint to use the config-conventional rules as the standard for linting[4] your commit messages.

Now, let's set up Git hooks so commitlint runs after you write a commit message.

Setting Up Husky

Install husky, which you will use to configure your project's Git hooks[5].

Figure 37. Command Line

```
1   npm i -D husky@9.1.7
```

---

[4]https://en.wikipedia.org/wiki/Lint_(software)
[5]https://www.atlassian.com/git/tutorials/git-hooks

• Husky is a tool that makes it easier and more efficient to work with Git hooks.
• Git hooks are scripts Git invokes automatically whenever certain events occur in the project you've initialized Git. For instance, a `pre-commit` hook is a script Git runs before committing your code. In contrast, a `post-commit` hook is a script that Git runs after you commit your code.

You need to set up Husky to work with Git hooks. Let's do that next.

Figure 38. Command Line

```
1   npx husky init
```

The command above tells Husky to do the following:

• Create a `.husky` directory in your project's root directory.
• Add a `pre-commit` script to the newly created `.husky` folder.
• Initialize the `pre-commit` hook with an `npm test` command that will run before Git commits your code.
• Add a `"prepare": "husky"` field to the `"scripts"` section in your package.json. This lets you run Husky with the `npm run prepare` command.

Now you can set up Husky to run `commitlint` every time you write a commit message.

Creating a Hook to Auto-Lint Commit Messages

The `commitlint/cli` package does not automatically lint commit messages. To enable this, add a Git `commit-msg` hook to your Husky workflow.

Figure 39. Command Line

```
1   echo 'npx --no -- commitlint --edit ${1}' > .husky/commit-msg
```

The command above does the following:

• Create a `commit-msg` script file in the `.husky` directory.

- Add the `npx --no -- commitlint --edit ${1}` command to the `commit-msg` hook so `commitlint` runs on every commit message.

 The syntax for the above echo code[6] is `echo text-to-write > file-to-write-into`.

Now, if you use `git commit -m` with a message that doesn't follow the format, `commitlint` will show an error. For example, try committing with a message that isn't conventional:

Figure 40. Command Line

```
1  git add -A && git commit -m "Install plugins to enforce conventional commits"
```

When you run the above commit command, `commitlint` will show an error like this:

Figure 41. Command Line

```
1      input: Install plugins to enforce conventional commits
2  ✖   subject may not be empty [subject-empty]
3  ✖   type may not be empty [type-empty]
4
5  ✖   found 2 problems, 0 warnings
6      Get help:
↪      https://github.com/conventional-changelog/commitlint/#what-is-commitlint
7
8  husky - commit-msg script failed (code 1)
```

`commitlint/cli` gave this error because the commit message didn't follow the rules. Let's fix it:

Figure 42. Command Line

```
1  git add -A && git commit -m "chore(commitlint): install plugins to enforce
↪      conventional commits"
```

The corrected commit command works without errors because it follows the Conventional Commits rules. You'll see a success message like this:

---

[6]https://codesweetly.com/how-to-use-git/#how-to-write-text-into-a-file-via-the-terminal

Figure 43. Command Line

```
1  [main 813dfc3] chore(commitlint): install plugins to enforce conventional
   ↪  commits
2  5 files changed, 737 insertions(+), 1 deletion(-)
3  create mode 100644 .husky/commit-msg
4  create mode 100644 .husky/pre-commit
5  create mode 100644 commitlint.config.ts
```

It's easy to skip standardized commit messages since Git hooks only work in your local project. Git does not copy hooks when you clone a repo, so hooks are not shared. And anyone with local access can change them, so developers can choose not to use standardized commit messages.

To make sure everyone on the team uses the same commit message format, set up GitHub Actions[7] in your CI/CD workflow. This approach ensures that only compliant commits can be pushed to the remote repository, promoting standardization across the team.

Let's look at how to set up the Commitlint GitHub Actions in the next chapter.

---

[7]https://www.youtube.com/watch?v=7pBcuT7j_A0&t=279s

Setting Up Commitlint GitHub Action

Below are the steps to add the Commitlint GitHub Action to your team's workflow.

1. Create a Commitlint GitHub Action Workflow File

Create a .github folder in your project's root directory, and add a /workflows/commitlint.yml file.

Figure 44. Command Line

```
1  mkdir .github && mkdir .github/workflows && touch
   ↪  .github/workflows/commitlint.yml
```

Here's what each command does:

- mkdir .github: Create a .github directory.
- mkdir .github/workflows: Create a workflows folder in the .github directory.
- touch .github/workflows/commitlint.yml: Create   a   commitlint.yml file inside the workflows directory.
- The && symbol means "and." It lets you chain several command-line commands.

2. Define the Commitlint GitHub Action Workflow

Open the new workflow file and add the following code:

Figure 45. commitlint.yml

```
1   name: Lint Commit Messages
2   on: [pull_request, push]
3
4   jobs:
5     commitlint:
6       runs-on: ubuntu-latest
7       steps:
8         - uses: actions/checkout@v6
9           with:
10            fetch-depth: 0
11        - uses: wagoid/commitlint-github-action@v6
```

The snippet above tells GitHub to use `commitlint` to lint commits from every pull request and push event.

 Proper indentation is required. The Commitlint GitHub Action work-flow[1] will only run successfully if the indentation is correct.

3. Test the Commitlint GitHub Action Workflow

Stage and commit your recent changes, ensuring the commit message follows the Conventional Commits format.

Figure 46. Command Line

```
1   git add -A && git commit -m "ci(github): create commitlint github action"
```

Next, push the commits to the remote repository:

Figure 47. Command Line

```
1   git push -u origin main
```

After pushing your commits, go to the "Actions" tab in your project's GitHub repository to view the workflow. Here is an example screenshot:

---

[1]https://github.com/wagoid/commitlint-github-action

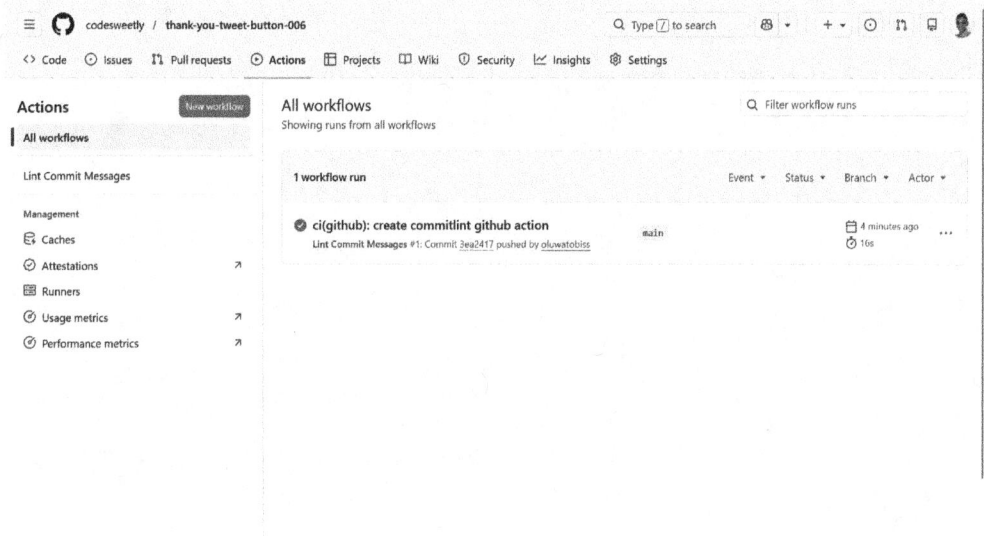

Figure 48. The Commitlint GitHub Action Workflow section of the Thank You Tweet Button GitHub repo

Now, let's add some styles to the `TweetButton` component.

Styling React Components

Below are the steps to style your package's React components.

1. Create the Stylesheet

Create a CSS file for the `TweetButton` component in the root directory:

Figure 49. Command Line

```
1  touch index.css
```

Afterward, open the newly created CSS file and declare your styles:

Figure 50. index.css

```
1   .tweet-btn-container {
2     margin-top: 30px;
3   }
4
5   .tweet-button {
6     display: inline-block;
7     text-decoration: none;
8     font-size: 0.97rem;
9     font-weight: bold;
10    color: #333;
11    background-color: #eee;
12    padding: 17px 35px;
13    border-radius: 7px;
14    border-block: 1px solid #ccc;
15    border-inline: 1px solid #333;
16  }
17
18  .tweet-button:hover {
19    text-decoration: none;
20    color: #fff;
21    background-color: #1a8cd8;
22    border-block-color: #1a8cd8;
23  }
```

Now, let's apply the styles to the component.

2. Apply CSS Styles to Your Component

Use the styles in your component:

Figure 51. TweetButton.jsx: Update 6-7

```
1  export function TweetButton() {
2    const tweetURL =
3      "https://twitter.com/intent/tweet?text=Thank+you,+%40oluwatobiss.+Your+bo⌐
   ↪    ok+helped+me+create,+test,+and+publish+an+NPM+package.%0A%0ACreating%⌐
   ↪    20NPM%20Package%0A%0Ahttps%3A%2F%2Famzn.to/4lifL3n";
4
5    return (
6      <div className="tweet-btn-container">
7        <a className="tweet-button" href={tweetURL} target="_blank">
8          Send a thank you tweet
9        </a>
10     </div>
11   );
12 }
```

3. Add the Stylesheet to the Entry File

Add the stylesheet as a build asset in your entry file.

Figure 52. index.js: Specify stylesheet as build asset (line 1)

```
1  import "./index.css";
2  export { TweetButton } from "./TweetButton";
```

The CSS import statement tells Vite to treat `index.css` as a build asset, ensuring it is processed and included in the `dist` folder.

 By default, Vite uses the `build.lib.fileName` field in `vite.config.js` as the compiled CSS filename. To change the default name, use `build.lib.cssFileName`.

4. Run the Test

Run your test code:

Figure 53. Command Line

```
1  npm run test
```

Once your test passes, stage and commit your changes:

Figure 54. Command Line

```
1  git add -A && git commit -m "style: create the tweet button's stylesheet"
```

Keep in mind that browsers can't read React directly. You need to convert your JSX into JavaScript that browsers understand. We'll cover how to do this in the next chapter.

Compiling React to JavaScript

To compile your React code to JavaScript, execute the Vite compilation command in the terminal:

Figure 55. Command Line

```
1  npx vite build
```

 When you use the npx command, the terminal searches for the vite executable in your project's local node_modules folder. This way, vite compiles your code with the project's local Vite version rather than the global one.

You can also add the compilation command to the "scripts" field of your project's package.json file:

Figure 56. package.json: Add build field (line 5)

```
1  {
2    "name": "thank-you-tweet-button-001",
3    "version": "1.0.0",
4    "scripts": {
5      "build": "vite build",
6      "test": "vitest run",
7      "prepare": "husky"
8    }
9  }
```

By so doing, you can compile the project from your terminal like this:

Figure 57. Command Line

```
1  npm run build
```

You do not need to use npx in the build script because NPM tem-
porarily adds ./node_modules/.bin/ to the beginning of the script's
path when running scripts from package.json. For example, NPM
runs ./node_modules/.bin/vite build automatically.

Right now, all your files are in the root folder. It's common to keep your
source code in a src directory and your compiled code in a dist folder. Let's
set it up this way too.

Source code vs. compiled code

- Source code is the original file you write and edit. Compilers like
  TypeScript's tsc command turn this source code into distribution
  code.
- Distribution code is the minified and optimized version of your source
  code. It's the JavaScript file the compiler creates for your project.

Distinguishing Source Code from Distribution Code

Begin by creating a src directory at the root of your package to clearly separate source code from distribution code.

Figure 58. Command Line

```
1    mkdir src
```

Next, move all JSX files, stylesheets, test files, and the package's entry point into the src folder.

Figure 59. Command Line

```
1    mv TweetButton.jsx index.css TweetButton.test.jsx index.js src/
```

It's a good idea to keep your components in their own folder. Create a components folder inside the src directory.

Figure 60. Command Line

```
1    mkdir src/components
```

Move your component files and related tests into the components folder.

Figure 61. Command Line

```
1    mv src/TweetButton.jsx src/TweetButton.test.jsx src/components/
```

Update the entry field in vite.config.js to reflect the revised project structure.

Figure 62. vite.config.js: Update entry field (line 15)

```
1   import react from "@vitejs/plugin-react";
2   import { defineConfig } from "vite";
3   import { resolve } from "path";
4   import { readFileSync } from "fs";
5
6   const pkg = JSON.parse(
7     readFileSync(new URL("./package.json", import.meta.url), "utf8"),
8   );
9   const peerDependenciesNames = Object.keys(pkg.peerDependencies || {});
10
11  export default defineConfig({
12    plugins: [react()],
13    build: {
14      lib: {
15        entry: resolve(import.meta.dirname, "src/index.js"),
16        formats: ["es", "cjs"],
17        fileName: "index",
18      },
19      rolldownOptions: {
20        external: (moduleSpecifier) => {
21          return peerDependenciesNames.some(
22            (name) =>
23              moduleSpecifier === name || moduleSpecifier.startsWith(`${name}/`),
24          );
25        },
26      },
27    },
28    test: {
29      environment: "jsdom",
30      globals: false,
31    },
32  });
```

Similarly, update the entry file to ensure that the module specifiers correspond to the new project structure.

Figure 63. index.js: Update the module specifiers (line 2)

```
1   import "./index.css";
2   export { TweetButton } from "./components/TweetButton";
```

Run the build process again.

Figure 64. Command Line

```
1   npm run build
```

You should also run your tests to make sure everything is working.

Figure 65. Command Line

```
1   npm run test
```

After that, stage and commit your recent changes.

Figure 66. Command Line

```
1   git add -A && git commit -m "build: distinguish source and distribution code"
```

In the next chapter, you'll learn how to set your package's entry point[1].

---

[1]https://codesweetly.com/web-tech-terms-e#entry-point

Defining Package's Runtime Entry Points

Since your package supports two different compilation targets (ECMAScript and CommonJS), ensure that tools that consume your package can detect and use either format as needed.

Use the `exports` field to define runtime entry points for both CommonJS and ECMAScript module consumers.

Figure 67. package.json: Create exports field (line 4-9)

```
1  {
2    "name": "thank-you-tweet-button-001",
3    "version": "1.0.0",
4    "exports": {
5      ".": {
6        "require": "./dist/index.cjs",
7        "import": "./dist/index.js"
8      }
9    },
10   "license": "ISC"
11 }
```

The `exports` field is the modern alternative to `main` and `module`. You may include these legacy fields to support Node.js 10 and earlier.

Figure 68. package.json: Include legacy main and module fields (line 4-5)

```
1  {
2    "name": "thank-you-tweet-button-001",
3    "version": "1.0.0",
4    "main": "./dist/index.cjs",
5    "module": "./dist/index.js",
6    "exports": {
7      ".": {
8        "require": "./dist/index.cjs",
9        "import": "./dist/index.js"
10     }
11   },
```

```
12      "license": "ISC"
13    }
```

With this setup, only tools that do not support `exports` will fall back to using the `main` and `modules` fields.

Now, stage and commit your recent changes.

Figure 69. Command Line

```
1   git add -A && git commit -m "chore: define package's entry point"
```

Also, make the stylesheet available as a public asset in your NPM package so users can import it directly into their projects.

Figure 70. package.json: Expose the project's stylesheet (line 11)

```
1   {
2     "name": "thank-you-tweet-button-001",
3     "version": "1.0.0",
4     "main": "./dist/index.cjs",
5     "module": "./dist/index.js",
6     "exports": {
7       ".": {
8         "require": "./dist/index.cjs",
9         "import": "./dist/index.js"
10      },
11      "./style.css": "./dist/index.css"
12    },
13    "license": "ISC"
14  }
```

 By default, Vite uses the `build.lib.fileName` field in `vite.config.js` as the compiled CSS filename. To change the default name, use `build.lib.cssFileName`.

When you use the explicit style export pattern, users can import the stylesheet into their projects like this:

Figure 71. Example of how users can import your NPM package's stylesheet into their application

```
1   import "thank-you-tweet-button-001/style.css";
```

 Letting users import styles directly helps avoid hidden side effects, like automatically loading unexpected global styles.

Stage and commit your latest changes.

Figure 72. Command Line

```
1   git add -A && git commit -m "style: export stylesheet as part of the package's
    ↪   public apis"
```

It's a good practice to test your package locally before publishing it to NPM. The next chapter will explain how to do this.

Local Testing of Unpublished Package

In this section, you'll use a Next.js project to learn how to test your package locally before publishing it to NPM.

 Next.js is just an example here. You can follow these steps with other React frameworks like Astro, Vite, or Gatsby. If you haven't used Next.js before, that's fine—only the basics are needed for testing.

Let's get started by link-installing your package globally.

1. Link-Install Your Package Globally in Your System

To test your unpublished package locally, first link-install it globally. Open your terminal, go to your project's root directory if you aren't there already, and create a symlink as shown below:

Figure 73. Command Line

```
1  npm link
```

The npm link[1] command creates a symlink (symbolic link[2]) in your system's global directory that points to your package.

- Make sure to run the command in the folder containing your package.json file. If you don't, the app might show a "Module Not Found" error when installing your package.
- You can use the npm ls --global command to check the location and contents of your global folder.

Let's now create the Next.js app you'll use to test your package.

---

[1]https://docs.npmjs.com/cli/v9/commands/npm-link
[2]https://en.wikipedia.org/wiki/Symbolic_link

2. Create a NextJS Demo Website for Testing Your Package

First, move out of your project's root directory and go to the folder where you want to set up the test app.

Then, initialize a Next.js app like so:

Figure 74. Command Line

```
1  npx create-next-app@16.2.4
```

Once you run the command, Next.js will ask you these questions:

- **Ok to proceed? (y)** Enter the y key on your keyboard to proceed.
- **What is your project named?** You may choose any name, such as `test-app-for-thank-you-tweet-button-001`.
- **Would you like to use the recommended Next.js defaults?** Select No, *customize settings* to customize the settings for your preferred setup.
- **Would you like to use TypeScript? » No / Yes** Select No, since this tutorial uses vanilla React + JavaScript only.
- **Which linter would you like to use?** Select *None*, because this tutorial doesn't use a linter.
- **Would you like to use React Compiler? » No / Yes** Select *Yes* to let React optimize your app's performance.
- **Would you like to use Tailwind CSS? » No / Yes** Select *No*, since this tutorial doesn't use Tailwind CSS.
- **Would you like your code inside a `src/` directory? » No / Yes** Select *No*, because this tutorial doesn't use a `src/` directory for the test app.
- **Would you like to use App Router? (recommended) » No / Yes** Select *Yes*, since we prefer using Next's App Router[3] settings. If you aren't familiar with App Router, that's okay, this tutorial only uses basic features to help you test your package.
- **Would you like to customize the import alias (@/* by default)? » No / Yes** Select *No* to keep Next.js's default import alias[4] for this test app.

---

[3]https://nextjs.org/docs/app
[4]https://dev.to/rhammy/path-aliases-in-nextjs-2fnc

- **Would you like to include AGENTS.md to guide coding agents to write up-to-date Next.js code? » No / Yes** Select No, as this guide does not use an AI coding assistant for the test app's codebase.

After you answer all the questions, Next.js will create your new app. Use the command line to go into the app directory:

Figure 75. Command Line

```
1  cd test-app-for-thank-you-tweet-button-001
```

Let's now install your package in the newly created React app.

3. Install Your Package from Your System's Global Folder to the Test-App

Go to your test app's root directory if you aren't there already, and create a symlink from the globally installed package to your NextJS demo app's node_-modules folder:

Figure 76. Command Line

```
1  npm link package-name
```

- Replace package-name with your package's name as listed in the name field of its package.json. For example: npm link thank-you-tweet-button-001.
- NPM will disconnect the symlink if you install or uninstall packages. If that happens, just run the npm link package-name command again.

After you run the command, NPM will link-install the package in your test app's node_modules folder.

4. Configure Turbopack to Resolve Symlinks

Next.js's Turbopack bundler looks for modules in your app's root directory and doesn't automatically find files outside the project. Because of this, it can't auto-resolve symlinks. To fix this, set `turbopack.root`[5] to the parent directory of both your Next.js app and the linked package:

Figure 77. next.config.js: Set turbopack's root option (line 1-6, 9-11)

```
1   import path from "path";
2   import { fileURLToPath } from "url";
3
4   const __filename = fileURLToPath(import.meta.url);
5   const __dirname = path.dirname(__filename);
6
7   /** @type {import('next').NextConfig} */
8   const nextConfig = {
9     turbopack: {
10      root: path.resolve(__dirname, "../"),
11    },
12    reactCompiler: true,
13  };
14
15  export default nextConfig;
```

The configuration above sets `turbopack.root` to the parent directory of both the Next.js app and the symlinked package. Here, the `../` path refers to the directory immediately above the test app's root directory.

Once the symlink is set up, you can use the library just like you would if you had published and installed it from NPM. For example, let's add the tweet button to your test app's homepage.

5. Use the Link-Installed Package in Your Test-App

Open the `page.js` file located in the `app` folder of your Next.js application.

---

[5]https://nextjs.org/docs/app/api-reference/config/next-config-js/turbopack#root-directory

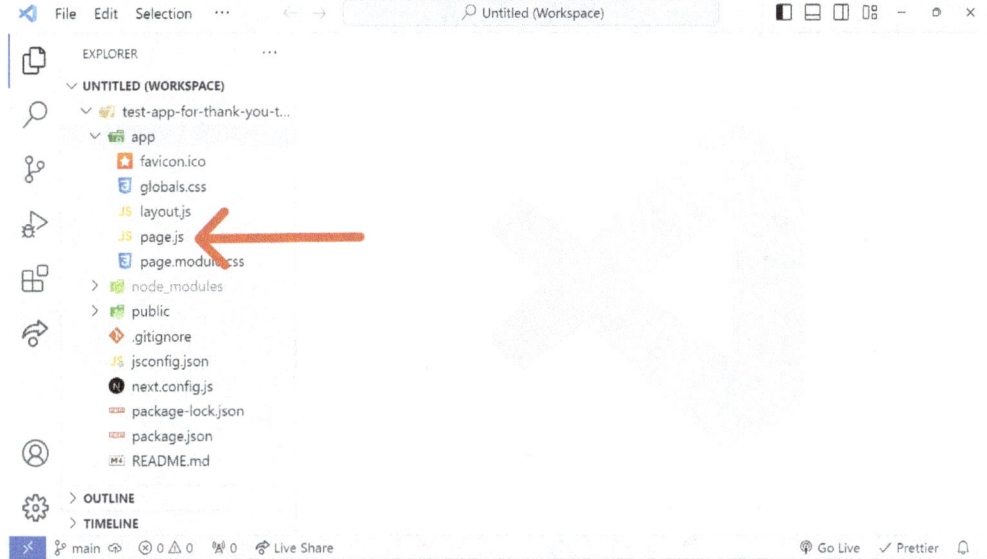

Figure 78. Red arrow pointing to the app directory's page.js file

Delete the file's content and paste in the following code:

Figure 79. page.js

```
1   import { TweetButton } from "thank-you-tweet-button-001";
2   import "thank-you-tweet-button-001/style.css";
3
4   export default function Home() {
5     return (
6       <main style={{ textAlign: "center", paddingTop: "30px" }}>
7         <h1>Hi there!</h1>
8         <TweetButton />
9       </main>
10    );
11  }
```

The snippet above does the following:

1. Imports the `TweetButton` component from the `thank-you-tweet-button-001` symlinked package.
2. Imports the `TweetButton` component's stylesheet.
3. Creates a `Home` component that renders a `<main>` element containing an `<h1>` node and your `<TweetButton>` component.

Next, run the test application as follows:

Figure 80. Command Line

```
1   npm run dev
```

 To stop the dev server's execution, use `ctrl + c` on windows or `cmd + c` on mac.

Note

Next.js may throw a `"TypeError: Super expression must either be null or a function"` error if any installed library uses event listeners or lifecycle effects such as `onClick()`, `onChange()`, `useState()`, and `useEffect()`. The error is because all Next's App Router components are Server Components by default[6].

To fix the error, add a "use client" directive at the top of the page, above all your import statements, like this:

Figure 81. page.js: Add use client directive (line 1)

```
1   "use client";
2
3   import { useState } from "react";
4   import { TweetButton } from "thank-you-tweet-button-001";
5   import "thank-you-tweet-button-001/style.css";
6
7   export default function Home() {
8     const [word, setWord] = useState("there");
9
10    return (
11      <main style={{ textAlign: "center", paddingTop: "30px" }}>
12        <h1>Hi {word}!</h1>
13        <TweetButton />
14      </main>
15    );
16  }
```

By doing so, Next.js will treat all modules imported into the page as Client Components.

When you're done developing and testing your package, you can unlink the symlinks with NPM. Here's how:

6. Unlink Your Package from the Test-App

Navigate to the root directory of your test app, where you imported and tested your package.

Figure 82. The Syntax to Change to a Different Directory

```
1   cd path/to/the-project-for-testing-the-package
```

Then, uninstall the package from your test app's `node_modules` folder:

Figure 83. Command Line

```
1   npm unlink package-name
```

 Replace `package-name` with the name of your package as defined in the `name` field of its `package.json`. For example: `npm unlink thank-you-tweet-button-001`.

After running the command above, NPM will remove the package from the test app's `node_modules` folder.

The next step is to uninstall the package from the global directory.

7. Unlink Your Package from the Global Folder

Run the following command on your terminal to uninstall the package from the global folder.

---

[6]https://nextjs.org/docs/app/building-your-application/rendering/client-components#using-client-components-in-nextjs

Figure 84. Command Line

```
1  npm rm --global package-name
```

- Replace `package-name` with the name of your package as defined in its `package.json`'s `"name"` field. For instance, `npm rm --global thank-you-tweet-button-001`.
- You can run the command above from any of your system's directories because the uninstallation occurs in the global directory.

Once you run the command, NPM will remove the package from your system's global folder.

Use the `npm ls --global package-name` command to confirm the package's removal from the global directory.

After creating and testing your package locally, proceed to document the library's purpose in a README file in the next chapter.

Creating README

A README file[1] documents the purpose of a software library. To create one, run the following command in your project's root directory:

Figure 85. Command Line

```
1   touch README.md
```

After creating the file, open it and provide the following information:

- A description of your package
- The problem it solves
- The package's key features
- A live demo link (if available)
- How to install it
- How to use it
- The dependencies it needs to run

Here's an example:

Figure 86. README.md

```
1    > **Note**
2    >
3    > This package is a project in the
4    [Creating NPM Package book](https://amzn.to/4lifL3n).
5
6    # Thank You Tweet Button 001
7
8    An easy-to-use tweet button for saying thank you to @oluwatobiss.
9
10   This button auto-fills your tweet pop-up modal with a nicely worded
11   thank you message.
12
13   ## Features
14
```

[1]https://www.makeareadme.com

```
15   - A button that posts a thank you message
16
17   ## Live Demo
18
19   https://codesweetly.com
20
21   ## Installation
22
23   This section shows how to install the Thank You Tweet Button 001
24   package.
25
26   ### Using npm
27
28   \`\`\`
29   npm install thank-you-tweet-button-001
30   \`\`\`
31
32   ### Using yarn
33
34   \`\`\`
35   yarn add thank-you-tweet-button-001
36   \`\`\`
37
38   ### Using pnpm
39
40   \`\`\`
41   pnpm add thank-you-tweet-button-001
42   \`\`\`
43
44   ## Usage
45
46   Import the library and its stylesheet, and use it as shown below:
47
48   \`\`\`jsx
49   import { TweetButton } from "thank-you-tweet-button-001";
50   import "thank-you-tweet-button-001/index.css";
51
52   function App() {
53   return <TweetButton />;
54   }
55   \`\`\`
56
57   ### Why import the stylesheet?
58
59   The components rely on predefined CSS classes for styling. Importing the
↪    stylesheet once ensures consistent application of these styles across all
↪    components.
60
61   ## Dependencies
62
```

```
63  - [React](https://github.com/facebook/react)
64
65  ## Dev Dependencies
66
67  - [Vite](https://github.com/vitejs/vite)
68  - [Vitest](https://github.com/vitest-dev/vitest)
69  - [React Testing Library]
70  (https://github.com/testing-library/react-testing-library)
```

Let's now stage and commit your recent changes:

Figure 87. Command Line

```
1  git add -A && git commit -m "docs: create project's readme"
```

In the next chapter, we'll create a license file, so others know what permissions they have to use your NPM package.

Creating LICENSE

Create a LICENSE file in your project's root directory as follows:

Figure 88. Command Line

```
1  touch LICENSE
```

Next, open the new file and add your chosen license text. For example, if you select the MIT open-source license, you can use the text provided on choosealicense.com[1].

Here's an example:

Figure 89. LICENSE

```
1   MIT License
2
3   Copyright (c) 2024-present FirstName LastName & Company
4   <username@yourdomain.com>
5
6   Permission is hereby granted, free of charge, to any person obtaining
7   a copy of this software and associated documentation files
8   (the "Software"), to deal in the Software without restriction,
9   including without limitation the rights to use, copy, modify, merge,
10  publish, distribute, sublicense, and/or sell copies of the Software,
11  and to permit persons to whom the Software is furnished to do so,
12  subject to the following conditions:
13
14  The above copyright notice and this permission notice shall be
15  included in all copies or substantial portions of the Software.
16
17  THE SOFTWARE IS PROVIDED "AS IS", WITHOUT WARRANTY OF ANY KIND,
18  EXPRESS OR IMPLIED, INCLUDING BUT NOT LIMITED TO THE WARRANTIES OF
19  MERCHANTABILITY, FITNESS FOR A PARTICULAR PURPOSE AND NONINFRINGEMENT.
20  IN NO EVENT SHALL THE AUTHORS OR COPYRIGHT HOLDERS BE LIABLE FOR ANY
21  CLAIM, DAMAGES OR OTHER LIABILITY, WHETHER IN AN ACTION OF CONTRACT,
22  TORT OR OTHERWISE, ARISING FROM, OUT OF OR IN CONNECTION WITH THE
23  SOFTWARE OR THE USE OR OTHER DEALINGS IN THE SOFTWARE.
```

Now, save and commit your latest changes:

---

[1]https://choosealicense.com/licenses/mit

Figure 90. Command Line

```
1   git add -A && git commit -m "docs: create project's license"
```

What happens if you don't provide a license?

Without a license or other agreement in place, any contributions are exclusively owned by their authors. That means nobody – not even you – can use, copy, distribute, or modify their contributions. – Open Source Guides[2]

In the next chapter, we will talk about how to publish your package so others can use it.

---

[2]https://opensource.guide/legal/#:~:text=Without%20a%20license%20or%20other%20agreement%20in%20place%2C%20any%20contributions%20are%20exclusively%20owned%20by%20their%20authors%2E%20That%20means%20nobody%20%E2%80%93%20not%20even%20you%20%E2%80%93%20can%20use%2C%20copy%2C%20distribute%2C%20or%20modify%20their%20contributions

Publishing Package to NPM

Below are the steps to share your package with the world!

1. Search Engine Optimization (SEO)

Add the following fields to your `package.json` file to improve search visibility and provide essential details about your package.

Description

Use the `"description"` field to describe your package.

Figure 91. package.json: Update description field (line 4)

```
1  {
2    "name": "thank-you-tweet-button-001",
3    "version": "1.0.0",
4    "description": "Easy-to-use tweet button for saying thank you to
   ↪ @oluwatobiss.",
5    "license": "ISC"
6  }
```

 The `description` property enhances your package's discoverability on the NPM website and is included in the results of the `npm search` command.

Keywords

Use the `keywords` field to specify key terms that accurately represent your package's functionality and intended use.

Here's an example:

Figure 92. package.json: Update keywords field (line 4-10)

```
1   {
2     "name": "thank-you-tweet-button-001",
3     "version": "1.0.0",
4     "keywords": [
5       "tweet",
6       "twitter",
7       "button",
8       "thank you",
9       "thanks"
10    ],
11    "description": "Easy-to-use tweet button for saying thank you to
          @oluwatobiss."
12  }
```

 The keywords property improves your package's visibility on the NPM website and is displayed in the output of the npm search command.

Author

Use the author field to include your name and contact information as the package author.

Figure 93. package.json: Update author field (line 4)

```
1   {
2     "name": "thank-you-tweet-button-001",
3     "version": "1.0.0",
4     "author": "Example Name <examplename@codesweetly.com>
          (https://www.codesweetly.com)",
5     "description": "Easy-to-use tweet button for saying thank you to
          @oluwatobiss."
6   }
```

An alternative way to define the "author" field is as follows:

Figure 94. package.json: Update author field (line 4-8)

```
1  {
2    "name": "thank-you-tweet-button-001",
3    "version": "1.0.0",
4    "author": {
5      "name": "Example Name",
6      "email": "examplename@codesweetly.com",
7      "url": "https://www.codesweetly.com"
8    },
9    "description": "Easy-to-use tweet button for saying thank you to
   ↪  @oluwatobiss."
10 }
```

License

Use the `license` field to indicate the licensing terms governing the use and distribution of your package.

Figure 95. package.json: Update license field (line 4)

```
1  {
2    "name": "thank-you-tweet-button-001",
3    "version": "1.0.0",
4    "license": "MIT",
5    "description": "Easy-to-use tweet button for saying thank you to
   ↪  @oluwatobiss."
6  }
```

Homepage

Use the `homepage` field to provide the URL of your package's official website or documentation.

Figure 96. package.json: Update homepage field (line 4)

```
1  {
2    "name": "thank-you-tweet-button-001",
3    "version": "1.0.0",
4    "homepage": "https://github.com/your-username/package-repo-name#readme",
5    "license": "MIT"
6  }
```

2. Confirm That Your Package Have Passing Tests

Make sure all your tests pass.

Figure 97. Command Line

```
1  npm run test
```

3. Compile Any Pending Code

Check that your latest code changes compile without any errors.

Figure 98. Command Line

```
1  npm run build
```

Let's now stage and commit your recent changes.

4. Stage and Commit Your Project's Changes to Git

Enter the following command on your terminal to stage and commit your recent changes.

Figure 99. Command Line

```
1  git add -A && git commit -m "chore: make package discoverable"
```

It is standard practice to publish only the files required for your package to function in production. This approach minimizes unnecessary downloads for users. So, let's also do the same.

5. Specify the Files You Want to Publish to NPM

Add a `"files"` field to your package.json and list the files you want to publish to NPM.

Here's an example:

Figure 100. package.json: Add files field (line 4-6)

```
1  {
2    "name": "thank-you-tweet-button-001",
3    "version": "1.0.0",
4    "files": [
5      "./dist"
6    ],
7    "license": "MIT"
8  }
```

NPM already includes these files by default, so you don't need to add them to the `"files"` field:

- package.json
- README
- LICENSE (LICENCE)
- The file in your package.json's `"main"` field

- Provide an empty array (`"files": []`) if the default files NPM includes are the only ones you want to publish.
- Omitting the files field will make NPM publish unnecessary files that users do not need to install and use your package.
- The NPM registry only works with folders that have a package.json file.

6. Confirm the Files NPM Will Publish

After you list the files to publish, it's a good idea to check them. Run the command below to see which files NPM will include.

Figure 101. Command Line

```
1   npm publish --dry-run
```

The above command instructs NPM to perform a dry run of the publication process, generating a report of the actions NPM will take when publishing the package.

You'll see a report like this:

Figure 102. Command Line

```
1   $ npm publish --dry-run
2
3   > thank-you-tweet-button-001@1.0.0 prepare
4   > husky
5
6   npm notice
7   npm notice   thank-you-tweet-button-001@1.0.0
8   npm notice Tarball Contents
9   npm notice 1.1kB LICENSE
10  npm notice 1.5kB README.md
11  npm notice 494B dist/index.cjs
12  npm notice 359B dist/index.css
13  npm notice 557B dist/index.js
14  npm notice 1.4kB package.json
15  npm notice Tarball Details
16  npm notice name: thank-you-tweet-button-001
17  npm notice version: 1.0.0
18  npm notice filename: thank-you-tweet-button-001-1.0.0.tgz
19  npm notice package size: 2.7 kB
20  npm notice unpacked size: 5.4 kB
21  npm notice shasum: e74187bcd2a461d2c944b0b62b54b6390cb040b1
22  npm notice integrity: sha512-rsX5wzfuINtGX[...]WPcu3XUzXfqhw==
23  npm notice total files: 6
24  npm notice
25  npm notice Publishing to https://registry.npmjs.org/ with tag latest and
    ↪   default access (dry-run)
26  + thank-you-tweet-button-001@1.0.0
```

The "Tarball Contents" section lists all the files NPM will publish.

 Learn more about how npm publishing works[1].

When you're happy with the report, move on to the next step.

7. Stage and Commit Any Recent Changes

Stage and commit your recent changes.

Figure 103. Command Line

```
1   git add -A && git commit -m "chore: specify files to publish to npm"
```

8. Push Your Local Git Directory to the Remote Repo

Upload your project to your git repository.

Figure 104. Command Line

```
1   git push -u origin main
```

9. Sign In or Sign Up on the NPM Website

Go to the NPM website[2] and sign in, or create an account if you don't have one yet.

 After creating a new account, verify your email. If you don't, you'll get a 403 Forbidden error when publishing.

10. Log In to NPM via the Terminal

Log in to your NPM account from the command line like this:

---

[1]https://blog.npmjs.org/post/165769683050/publishing-what-you-mean-to-publish
[2]https://www.npmjs.com

Figure 105. Command Line

```
1   npm login
```

 Run npm whoami to see if you're logged in.

11. Confirm If Your Package's Name Is Available

There are two main ways to check if your package's name is already taken.

1. CLI command

Use the following command to see if your package name is available.

Figure 106. Command Line

```
1   npm search package-name
```

 Replace package-name with the name of your package as defined in its package.json's "name" field. For instance, npm search thank-you-tweet-button-001.

If the name is available, it will not show up in the list of packages, or you might see a message saying 'No matches found for "your-package-name"'.

2. URL search

You can also check if your package name is available by searching for it on the NPM website or entering the following in your browser's address bar.

Figure 107. The URL Syntax to Search for a Package in the Browser's Address Bar

```
1  https://registry.npmjs.org/package-name
```

 Replace `package-name` with the name of your package as defined in its `package.json`'s `"name"` field. For instance, `https://registry.npmjs.org/thank-you-tweet-button-001`.

If you see `0 packages found` or `{"error": "Not found"}`, the name is available.

What to do if your chosen package name is currently in use by someone else

If all suitable names are unavailable, NPM allows you to publish your project under a user or organization scope.

This lets you publish your package under your NPM username as a sub-namespace. To do this, open your `package.json` and add your username before the package name.

Here's an example:

Figure 108. package.json: Update name field (line 2)

```
1  {
2    "name": "@yourusername/thank-you-tweet-button-001",
3    "version": "1.0.0"
4  }
```

Now, let's publish the package!

12. Publish Your Package!

Navigate to the root directory of your package and execute the following command to publish it:

Figure 109. Command Line

```
1   npm publish
```

 Type   https://www.npmjs.com/package/package-name   in your browser's address bar to see your package's homepage. (Note: Replace package-name with the name of your package as defined in its package.json's "name" field.   For instance, https://www.npmjs.com/package/thank-you-tweet-button-001.)

Did you get an error?

If you used a scoped package name, NPM assumes it's private by default. You'll get an error if you try to publish it without changing this.

To publish a scoped package publicly, add --access=public to your npm publish command:

Figure 110. Command Line

```
1   npm publish --access=public
```

 You can make your project a scoped package during initialization by running npm init --scope=username instead of npm init.

After you publish to NPM, it's a good idea to test the live package. We'll cover that in the next chapter.

Local Testing of the Published Package

Here are the steps to test your live package.

1. Install the Package

Open your terminal, go to your NextJS test app's root folder, and install your package.

Figure 111. Command Line

```
1   npm install package-name --save
```

 Replace `package-name` with the actual name of the package as specified in the `name` field of its `package.json` file. For example, use `npm install thank-you-tweet-button-001 --save`.

2. Import the Package

Open the `page.js` file located in the `app` folder of your Next.js application.

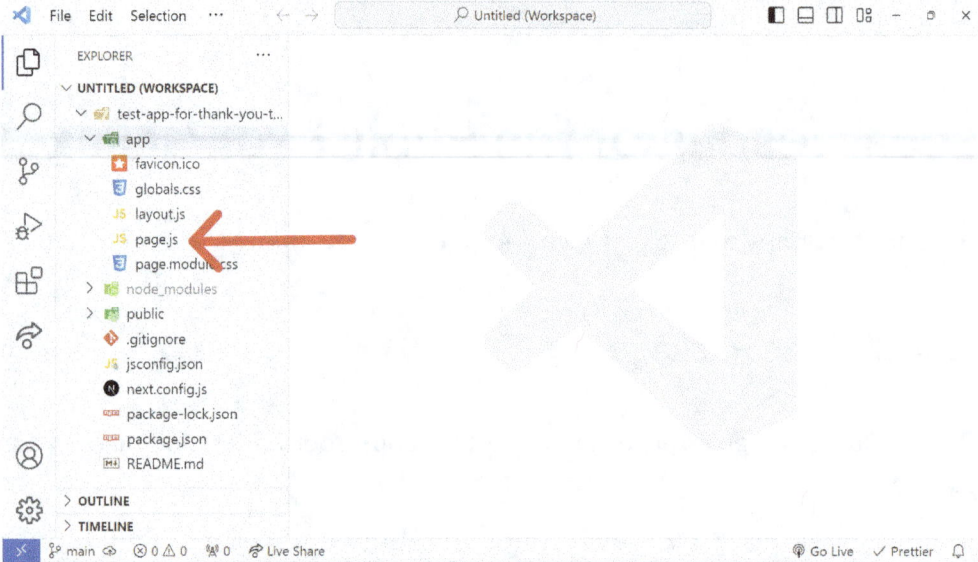

Figure 112. Red arrow pointing to the app directory's page.js file

Next, import and use the package like this:

Figure 113. page.js

```
1  import { TweetButton } from "thank-you-tweet-button-001";
2  import "thank-you-tweet-button-001/style.css";
3
4  export default function Home() {
5    return (
6      <main style={{ textAlign: "center", paddingTop: "30px" }}>
7        <h1>Hi there!</h1>
8        <TweetButton />
9      </main>
10   );
11 }
```

3. Run Your Local Server

Run the test application in the browser to verify that the package functions as intended.

Figure 114. Command Line

```
1  npm run dev
```

 To stop the dev server's execution, use `ctrl + c` on windows or `cmd + c` on mac.

Up to this point, you've tested the package locally. It's also a good idea to test it on a live server. In the next chapter, we'll do this using Vercel.

Production Testing of the Published Package

Here's how to test your live package on a website hosted with Vercel.

1. Stage and Commit Your Changes

Stage and commit the recent changes to your Next.js test app:

Figure 115. Command Line

```
1   git add -A && git commit -m "Add tweet button"
```

2. Set up a GitHub Remote Repository for Your Next.js Test App

1. Log in to your GitHub account.
2. Create a new GitHub repository for your Next.js demo website. You can name it `test-app-for-thank-you-tweet-button-001` or choose any name you like.
3. Link your demo website's local `.git` directory to the remote GitHub repository:

Figure 116. Command Line

```
1   git remote add origin https://github.com/your-username/remote-repo-name.git
```

 Replace `your-username` with your GitHub username and `remote-repo-name` with your repository's name.

3. Push Your Local Git Directory to the Remote Repo

Upload your Next.js test app project to your GitHub repository as follows:

Figure 117. Command Line

```
1   git push -u origin main
```

4. Sign In or Create an Account on the Vercel Website

Visit the Vercel website[1] and log in or sign up with your GitHub account.

 Use the GitHub account that hosts your Next.js test app project to sign in or sign up for Vercel.

5. Deploy Your Project to Vercel

1. Once you're in the Vercel dashboard, click the "Add New" button.
2. Then select the "Project" option from the dropdown menu.
3. You'll see a list of Git repositories under "Import Git Repository." Click the "Import" button next to the project you want to deploy.
4. Now click the "Deploy" button on the "New Project" page to launch your demo app.

 Because your Next.js demo website's GitHub repo is connected to Vercel, Vercel will automatically redeploy your test app whenever you push changes to GitHub.

---

[1]https://vercel.com

6. Test the Package on Your Live Demo Website

1. After you've deployed the demo website, click the "Continue to Dashboard" button on the congratulations screen.
2. Next, click the "Visit" button to open your deployed demo website.
3. When the demo app opens in your browser, try the Tweet button to make sure it works.

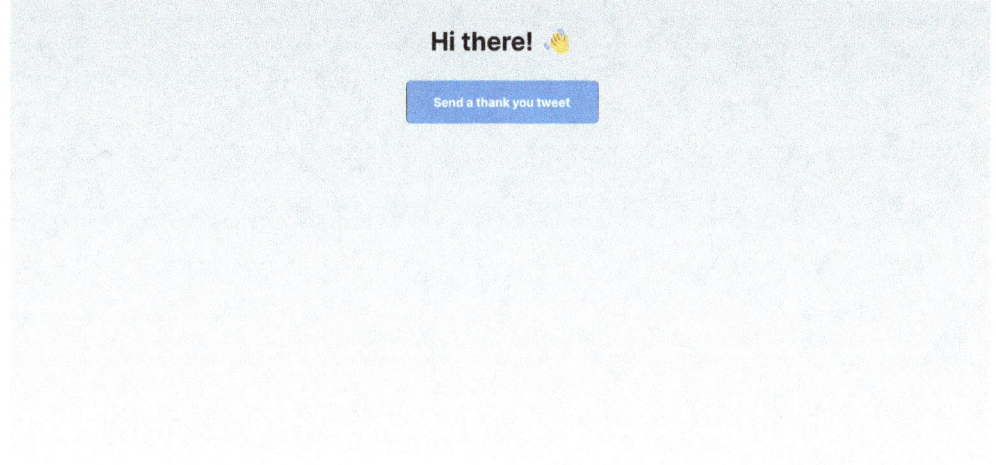

Figure 118. Tweet Button with a 'Send a thank you tweet' text

Congratulations! You now have a live NPM package running on a server. In the next chapter, you'll learn how to update the package's version number when you make important changes.

Updating Package's Versions

It's a good practice to update your package's version number whenever you make a significant change. This helps users see what kind of changes each release includes.

Here is the syntax for updating your package's version number:

Figure 119. The Syntax for Updating a Package's Version

```
1  npm version update-type
```

The command above tells NPM to update your package's version number to the specified `update-type`.

Note

- Replace `update-type` with the appropriate semantic versioning[1] release type: `patch`, `minor`, or `major`.
- Use `patch` for backward-compatible changes that do not add new features.
- Use `minor` when adding new features that remain backward-compatible.
- Use `major` for updates that break backward compatibility.
- Backward compatibility means the new version can use all the same APIs as the previous one without causing errors.

Now, let's look at some examples.

- Log in to your NPM account using `npm login` from the command line. If you do not, NPM will display an `Access token expired or revoked. Please try logging in again.` warning and prevent you from publishing.
- Run `npm whoami` to see if you're logged in.

---

[1]https://docs.npmjs.com/about-semantic-versioning

Example 1: Updating to a Patch Version

To update your package to a patch version, open your `TweetButton` component file and change the `<div>` element to a `<section>` element as shown
below:

Figure 120. TweetButton.jsx: Update line 6, 10

```
1   export function TweetButton() {
2     const tweetURL =
3       "https://twitter.com/intent/tweet?text=Thank+you,+%40oluwatobiss.+Your+bo⌐
      ↪  ok+helped+me+create,+test,+and+publish+an+NPM+package.%0A%0ACreating%⌐
      ↪  20NPM%20Package%0A%0Ahttps%3A%2F%2Famzn.to/4lifL3n";
4
5     return (
6       <section className="tweet-btn-container">
7         <a className="tweet-button" href={tweetURL} target="_blank">
8           Send a thank you tweet
9         </a>
10      </section>
11    );
12  }
```

This change counts as a `patch` update because:

1. We didn't add any new features.
2. The changes also don't break compatibility with the previous version.

After updating your code, run your build step:

Figure 121. Command Line

```
1   npm run build
```

 Test your updated package locally before committing your changes.
Refer to Chapter 10: Local Testing of Unpublished Package on page
45 to review the required steps.

When you're ready to save your changes, make a commit:

Figure 122. Command Line

```
1   git add -A && git commit -m "refactor: change div to section element"
```

Since this is a patch change, update your package's version like this:

Figure 123. Command Line

```
1   npm version patch
```

As a result, NPM will:

1. Increase the third digit in your `package.json`'s `"version"` field. For example, it will go from `"1.0.0"` to `"1.0.1"`.
2. Auto-commit the version update.
3. Create a Git tag for the new version. A Git tag[2] marks an important point in your project's history, like a package release. Use the `git tag` command to see all tags in your local repository.

Next, upload your recent commits to your git repository.

Figure 124. Command Line

```
1   git push -u origin main --tags
```

 The `--tags` flag ensures that all tags are pushed to the remote repository. By default, `git push` does not transfer tags.

Then, publish the latest version of your package:

Figure 125. Command Line

```
1   npm publish
```

---

[2]https://git-scm.com/book/en/v2/Git-Basics-Tagging

Now is an excellent time to test the patch publication with your NextJS demo website. Remember to update the test-app to the current version before running your tests. For instance, run `npm install thank-you-tweet-button-001@latest`.

Now, let's make a minor update.

Example 2: Updating to a Minor Version

To update your package to a minor version, open your `TweetButton` component file and add a new prop like this:

Figure 126. TweetButton.jsx

```
1  export function TweetButton(props) {
2    const tweetURL = `https://twitter.com/intent/tweet?text=Thank+you,+%40oluwa⌐
    ↪  tobiss.+Your+book+helped+me+create,+test,+and+publish+${
3      props.number && props.number > 1 ? props.number : "an"
4    }+NPM+${
5      props.number && props.number > 1 ? "packages" : "package"
6    }.%0A%0ACreating%20NPM%20Package%0A%0Ahttps%3A%2F%2Famzn.to/4lifL3n`;
7
8    return (
9      <section className="tweet-btn-container">
10       <a className="tweet-button" href={tweetURL} target="_blank">
11         Send a thank you tweet
12       </a>
13     </section>
14   );
15 }
```

 The `props.number && props.number > 1 ? props.number : "an"` code uses the following concepts:

- AND logical operator[3]
- Chained ternary operator[4]

This change is a `minor` update because:

---

[3]https://codesweetly.com/javascript-logic#and-operator-
[4]https://codesweetly.com/javascript-statement#what-is-a-chained-ternary-operator

1. We're adding a new feature (the `number` prop).
2. These changes don't break compatibility with the previous version. Users don't need to change their code to use this minor version. Anyone using the package without `props` can keep doing so. This update just adds a new optional feature.

So, after you build and publish the minor update, users will have two ways to use the `TweetButton` package:

First option (without props):

Figure 127. page.js: Invoke TweetButton without props (line 8)

```
1  import { TweetButton } from "thank-you-tweet-button-001";
2  import "thank-you-tweet-button-001/style.css";
3
4  export default function Home() {
5    return (
6      <main style={{ textAlign: "center", paddingTop: "30px" }}>
7        <h1>Hi there!</h1>
8        <TweetButton />
9      </main>
10   );
11 }
```

Second option (with props):

Figure 128. page.js: Invoke TweetButton with props (line 8)

```
1  import { TweetButton } from "thank-you-tweet-button-001";
2  import "thank-you-tweet-button-001/style.css";
3
4  export default function Home() {
5    return (
6      <main style={{ textAlign: "center", paddingTop: "30px" }}>
7        <h1>Hi there!</h1>
8        <TweetButton number={3} />
9      </main>
10   );
11 }
```

After updating your `TweetButton.jsx` code, run your build step:

Figure 129. Command Line

```
1   npm run build
```

 Test your updated package locally before committing your changes. Refer to Chapter 10: Local Testing of Unpublished Package on page 45 if you need to review the required steps.

When you're ready to save your changes, make a commit like this:

Figure 130. Command Line

```
1   git add -A && git commit -m "feat: allow users to specify the number of
    ↪   published packages"
```

Since this is a minor change, update your package's version like this:

Figure 131. Command Line

```
1   npm version minor
```

As a result, NPM will:

1. Increase the second digit in your `package.json`'s `"version"` field.
2. Reset the third digit to zero. For example, it will go from `"1.0.1"` to `"1.1.0"`.
3. Auto-commit the version update.
4. Create a Git tag for the new version. A Git tag marks an important point in your project's history, like a package release. Use the `git tag` command to see all tags in your local repository.

Next, upload your recent commits to your git repository.

Figure 132. Command Line

```
1   git push -u origin main --tags
```

The `--tags` flag ensures that all tags are pushed to the remote repository. By default, `git push` does not transfer tags.

Then, publish the latest version of your package:

Figure 133. Command Line

```
1   npm publish
```

 Now is an excellent time to test the minor publication with your NextJS demo website. Remember to update the test-app to the current version before running your tests. For instance, run `npm install thank-you-tweet-button-001@latest`.

Now, let's make a major update.

Example 3: Updating to a Major Version

To update your package to a major version, open your `TweetButton` component file and add a second prop like this:

Figure 134. TweetButton.jsx

```
1   function generateStarIcons(rating) {
2     const megaStars = `⭐⭐⭐⭐⭐ x ${Math.round(rating / 5)}`;
3     let stars = "";
4     for (let i = 0; i < rating; i++) {
5       stars += "⭐";
6     }
7     return rating > 10 ? megaStars : stars;
8   }
9
10  export function TweetButton(props) {
11    const tweetURL = `https://twitter.com/intent/tweet?text=Thank+you,+%40oluwa⌐
      ↪  tobiss.+Your+book+helped+me+create,+test,+and+publish+${
12      props.number && props.number > 1 ? props.number : "an"
13    }+NPM+${
14      props.number && props.number > 1 ? "packages" : "package"
15    }.%0A%0ABook's+Rating:+${props.rating}-star+rating!+${generateStarIcons(
16      props.rating,
17    )}+%0A%0ACreating%20NPM%20Package%0A%0Ahttps%3A%2F%2Famzn.to/4lifL3n`;
```

```
18
19      return props.rating ? (
20        <section className="tweet-btn-container">
21          <a className="tweet-button" href={tweetURL} target="_blank">
22            Send a thank you tweet
23          </a>
24        </section>
25      ) : (
26        <div
27          style={{
28            display: "flex",
29            justifyContent: "center",
30            marginTop: "30px",
31          }}
32        >
33          <p
34            style={{
35              backgroundColor: "#DC3545",
36              color: "#fff",
37              width: "35%",
38              borderRadius: "5px",
39              padding: "15px 20px",
40            }}
41          >
42            Error: Props 'rating' is missing in 'TweetButtonProps'.
43          </p>
44        </div>
45      );
46    }
```

This change is a major update because:

1. We're adding a new feature (the rating prop).
2. These changes break compatibility with the previous version of the package.

 The update introduced a breaking change because the package previously allowed users to use the <TweetButton /> API without any
required argument. But they must now provide a rating argument
(<TweetButton rating={value} />) for the library to work correctly. Otherwise, the component will issue an error.

You also need to update the test with the required props. So, open your test
file and add the rating prop as follows:

Figure 135. TweetButton.test.jsx: Add rating prop (line 6)

```
1  import { test } from "vitest";
2  import { render } from "@testing-library/react";
3  import { TweetButton } from "./TweetButton";
4
5  test("tweet button renders correctly", () => {
6    render(<TweetButton rating={35} />);
7  });
```

After updating your code, run the test:

Figure 136. Command Line

```
1  npm run test
```

Once your test passes, go ahead and run your build step:

Figure 137. Command Line

```
1  npm run build
```

 Test your updated package locally before committing your changes. Refer to Chapter 10: Local Testing of Unpublished Package on page 45 if you need to review the required steps.

When you're ready to save your changes, make a commit like this:

Figure 138. Command Line

```
1  git add -A && git commit -m "feat: make users provide a rating" -m "BREAKING
   ↪  CHANGE: This commit breaks compatibility with the previous version"
```

Note

- Each -m flag tells Git to begin a new paragraph.
- The first -m begins the commit message's header.
- The second -m begins the message's body.
- Starting the body with a BREAKING CHANGE text is one way to indicate

a breaking change in a commit. We will discuss an alternative method later in this book.

Since this is a major change, update your package's version like this:

Figure 139. Command Line

```
1   npm version major
```

As a result, NPM will:

1. Increase the first digit in your `package.json`'s `"version"` field.
2. Reset the second and third digits to zero. For example, it will go from `"1.1.0"` to `"2.0.0"`.
3. Auto-commit the version update.
4. Create a Git tag for the new version. A Git tag marks an important point in your project's history, like a package release. Use the `git tag` command to see all tags in your local repository.

Next, upload your recent commits to your Git repository.

Figure 140. Command Line

```
1   git push -u origin main --tags
```

The `--tags` flag ensures that all tags are pushed to the remote repository. By default, `git push` does not transfer tags.

Then, publish the latest version of your package:

Figure 141. Command Line

```
1   npm publish
```

Now is an excellent time to test the major publication with your NextJS demo website. Remember to update the test-app to the current version before running your tests. For instance, run `npm install thank-you-tweet-button-001@latest`.

The `npm version update-type` command works fine for minor updates, but automating the versioning process is even better. We'll talk about how to do that in the next chapter.

Automating Version Management

The following steps explain how to use GitHub Actions Workflow and the semantic-release[1] library to automate your package's version updates.

1. Create a Release GitHub Action Workflow File

Add a `/workflows/release.yml` file to your project's `.github/workflows` directory.

Figure 142. Command Line

```
1  touch .github/workflows/release.yml
```

The snippet above creates a `release.yml` file inside the `workflows` directory.

2. Define the Release GitHub Action Workflow

Open your new workflow file and paste in the following code:

Figure 143. release.yml

```
1  name: Release
2
3  on:
4    push:
5      branches:
6        - main
7
8  permissions:
9    id-token: write
10   contents: write
11
12 jobs:
```

---

[1]https://github.com/semantic-release/semantic-release

```
13    release:
14      name: Semantic Release
15      runs-on: ubuntu-latest
16      steps:
17        - name: Checkout repository
18          uses: actions/checkout@v6
19          with:
20            fetch-depth: 0
21            persist-credentials: false
22
23        - name: Setup Node.js
24          uses: actions/setup-node@v6
25          with:
26            node-version: 24
27            registry-url: https://registry.npmjs.org
28
29        - name: Install semantic-release
30          run: |
31            npm install --no-save \
32              semantic-release@25 \
33
34        - name: Build package
35          run: npm run build
36
37        - name: Run semantic-release
38          env:
39            GITHUB_TOKEN: ${{ secrets.GITHUB_TOKEN }}
40          run: npx semantic-release
```

Here's what the code above does:

- on: Tells GitHub to run the Release workflow only when you push to the main branch.
- permissions: Sets what the auto-generated GITHUB_TOKEN for the Release workflow is allowed to do:
    - id-token: write: Lets the token request a GitHub OIDC JWT, which NPM uses to check that your GitHub repo is allowed to publish the package.
    - contents: write: Lets the token make changes to your package's GitHub repo, like creating tags, releases, and fetching the full Git history.
- jobs: Lists the tasks for the workflow. In the example above, there's just the release job, which includes these steps:
    - Checkout (download) your project repository onto the server running the workflow, so the next steps can access the needed project files.

- Install and set up the specified Node.js version.
- Install `semantic-release`. Note: The `--no-save` flag keeps NPM from adding the installed packages to your `package.json` dependencies, so the workflow installs them only in the CI environment, not on your local machine.
- Run the `build` script to create a new `dist` directory for compiled files.
- Run `semantic-release` to automate the release process, using the GitHub App token for authentication.

- Ensure proper indentation, as the Commitlint GitHub Action workflow[2] requires correct indentation to execute successfully.
- The `fetch-depth: 0` property in the checkout step is required for semantic-release to analyze the full commit history and determine the next version.

The `semantic-release` package includes default options[3] that you can override. The following section explains how to do this.

3. How to Overwrite semantic-release's Default Configurations

Create a `.releaserc.mjs` configuration file in your project's root directory to change some of `semantic-release`'s default options.

Figure 144. Command Line

```
1   touch .releaserc.mjs
```

After you create the configuration file, open it and add the options you want to override.

Here's an example:

---

[2]https://github.com/wagoid/commitlint-github-action
[3]https://semantic-release.gitbook.io/semantic-release/usage/configuration

Figure 145. .releaserc.mjs

```
1    /**
2     * @type {import('semantic-release').GlobalConfig}
3     */
4    export default {
5      branches: ["main"],
6      repositoryUrl: "https://github.com/your-username/package-repo-name",
7      plugins: [
8        [
9          "@semantic-release/commit-analyzer",
10         {
11           preset: "conventionalcommits",
12           parserOpts: {
13             noteKeywords: ["BREAKING CHANGE", "BREAKING CHANGES"],
14           },
15           releaseRules: [
16             { breaking: true, release: "major" },
17             { type: "feat", release: "minor" },
18             { type: "fix", release: "patch" },
19             { type: "perf", release: "patch" },
20             { type: "refactor", release: "patch" },
21             { type: "docs", release: "patch" },
22             { type: "style", release: "patch" },
23             { type: "test", release: false },
24             { type: "chore", release: false },
25             { type: "ci", release: false },
26           ],
27         },
28       ],
29       ["@semantic-release/npm", { npmPublish: true }],
30     ],
31   };
```

> ℹ️ Replace `your-username` in the code above with your GitHub username. Likewise, replace `package-repo-name` with your remote repository's name. For example, `https://github.com/codesweetly/thank-you-tweet-button-001`.

The configuration above changes the default settings for the plugins that `semantic-release` uses during the release workflow.

- `branches`: Specify the branches where you want release automation to run.

- repositoryUrl: Provide your package's GitHub repository URL so semantic-release can connect to the correct remote repository.
- @semantic-release/commit-analyzer: Analyzes your commits and uses the releaseRules option to determine if a release is necessary and the next version number.
- @semantic-release/npm: Publishes the new package version to NPM.

- semantic-release will execute the plugins in the order you listed them in the plugins array.
- The plugins array overrides the default, so make sure you explicitly list all the plugins you want to use, including the default ones.
- Make sure to define the { breaking: true, release: "major" } release rule before other rules. This way, semantic-release always checks for breaking changes first. If not, breaking markers will be ignored.

4. Notify Developers That the Package Uses Automated Version Management

Update the package's version field to 0.0.0-development.

Figure 146. package.json: Update version field (line 3)

```
1  {
2    "name": "thank-you-tweet-button-001",
3    "version": "0.0.0-development",
4    "scripts": {
5      "build": "vite build",
6      "test": "vitest run",
7      "prepare": "husky"
8    }
9  }
```

Setting the version option to 0.0.0-development signals to developers and tools that this value is a placeholder and should not be used. An automated tool assigns the correct version during the publishing process.

The `@semantic-release/npm` plugin determines the new version based on your project's Git history and tags, rather than the `package.json` version number[4]. It updates the `version` field only in the published `package.json` and does not push this change to your GitHub repository.

After you set up `semantic-release` to automatically handle your package version bump, go ahead and commit your changes.

Figure 147. Command Line

```
1  git add -A && git commit -m "ci(semantic-release): automate package's version
   ↳   management"
```

To let your Release GitHub Action workflow publish your package to the NPM registry, you need to set up NPM to trust the workflow. We'll explain how to do this in the next chapter.

---

[4]https://github.com/semantic-release/semantic-release/blob/master/docs/support/ FAQ.md#it-is-not-needed-for-semantic-release-to-do-its-job

NPM Trusted Publishing Configuration

Follow the steps below to make sure NPM recognizes your library's GitHub repository as a trusted publisher for the NPM registry.

1. Go to your package's main page on the NPM website and click the "Settings" tab.
2. In the "Trusted Publisher" section, click the "GitHub Actions" button.
3. Fill in the following fields:

   - **Organization or user:** Enter the GitHub username or organization name associated with your package, for example, `codesweetly`.
   - **Repository:** Enter your package's GitHub repository, for example, `thank-you-tweet-button-001`.
   - **Workflow filename:** Enter the name of your release workflow file, for example, `release.yml`.

4. Click the "Set up connection" button to complete the configuration.

With this setup, NPM will recognize your repository as the only trusted publisher for your package. Let's test it.

Add a New Feature

Add a third prop to the TweetButton component.

Figure 148. TweetButton.jsx

```
1   function generateStarIcons(rating) {
2     const megaStars = `⭐⭐⭐⭐⭐ x ${Math.round(rating / 5)}`;
3     let stars = "";
4     for (let i = 0; i < rating; i++) {
5       stars += "⭐";
6     }
7     return rating > 10 ? megaStars : stars;
8   }
9
10  export function TweetButton(props) {
11    const tweetURL = `https://twitter.com/intent/tweet?text=Thank+you,+%40oluwa
    ↪   tobiss.+Your+book+helped+me+create,+test,+and+publish+${
12      props.number && props.number > 1 ? props.number : "an"
13    }+NPM+${
14      props.number && props.number > 1 ? "packages" : "package"
15    }.%0A%0AMy+Favorite:+${props.bestNPMPackage}%0A%0ABook's+Rating:+${
16      props.rating
17    }-star+rating!+${generateStarIcons(
18      props.rating
19    )}+%0A%0ACreating%20NPM%20Package%0A%0Ahttps%3A%2F%2Famzn.to/4lifL3n`;
20
21    return props.rating && props.bestNPMPackage ? (
22      <section className="tweet-btn-container">
23        <a className="tweet-button" href={tweetURL} target="_blank">
24          Send a thank you tweet
25        </a>
26      </section>
27    ) : (
28      <div
29        style={{
30          display: "flex",
31          justifyContent: "center",
32          marginTop: "30px",
33        }}
34      >
35        <p
36          style={{
37            backgroundColor: "#DC3545",
38            color: "#fff",
39            width: "35%",
40            borderRadius: "5px",
41            padding: "15px 20px",
42          }}
43        >
44          Error: One or more required props are missing in 'TweetButtonProps'.
45        </p>
46      </div>
47    );
```

```
48  }
```

This change is a `major` update because:

1. It adds a new feature: the `bestNPMPackage` prop.
2. It breaks compatibility with the previous version of the package.

 The update introduced a breaking change because the package previously allowed users to use the `<TweetButton />` API with only one required prop. But they must now provide two props (`<TweetButton rating={value} bestNPMPackage="value" />`) for the library to work correctly. Otherwise, the component will issue an error.

You also need to add the second required prop to the test script. Open your test file and add the `bestNPMPackage` prop as shown below:

Figure 149. TweetButton.test.jsx: Add bestNPMPackage prop (line 6)

```jsx
1  import { test } from "vitest";
2  import { render } from "@testing-library/react";
3  import { TweetButton } from "./TweetButton";
4
5  test("tweet button renders correctly", () => {
6    render(<TweetButton rating={37} bestNPMPackage="React YouTube Playlist" />);
7  });
```

After you update your code, run your test:

Figure 150. Command Line

```
1  npm run test
```

When the test passes, run the build step:

Figure 151. Command Line

```
1  npm run build
```

Test your updated package locally before you commit your changes. If you need a reminder of the steps, see Chapter 10: Local Testing of Unpublished Package on page 45.

When ready to save your changes, run a commit:

Figure 152. Command Line

```
1   git add -A && git commit -m 'feat(tweetbutton)!: make users to specify the best
 ↪   npm package they have created'
```

- The exclamation (!) means breaking change.
- Use single quotes (' ') whenever you use the exclamation mark in your commit message. Otherwise, bash will issue an "unrecognized history modifier" error.

Next, push the commits to the remote repository to release the latest version.

Figure 153. Command Line

```
1   git push -u origin main --tags
```

 The `--tags` flag is optional if the tags on the remote repository already match those on your local repository.

After you push your commits, go to the "Actions" tab in your project's GitHub repo to see the release workflow. Here's a screenshot from my project:

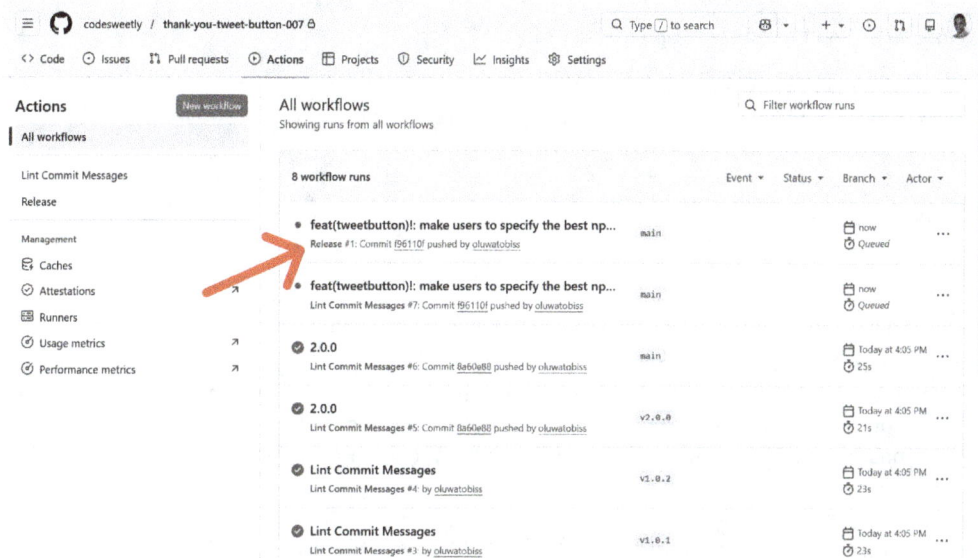

Figure 154. The Release GitHub Actions Workflow of the Thank You Tweet Button package

To see the latest version of your package in the NPM registry, go to `https://www.npmjs.com/package/package-name` in your browser. Be sure to replace `package-name` with the name of your package as defined in its `package.json`'s "name" field. For example: `https://www.npmjs.com/package/thank-you-tweet-button-001`.

Let's also update the button's `"Send"` text to `"Post"`.

Update an Existing Feature

Open your `TweetButton.tsx` file and update the button's `"Send"` text to `"Post"`.

Figure 155. TweetButton.jsx: Update line 24

```
1   function generateStarIcons(rating) {
2     const megaStars = `⭐⭐⭐⭐⭐ x ${Math.round(rating / 5)}`;
3     let stars = "";
4     for (let i = 0; i < rating; i++) {
5       stars += "⭐";
6     }
7     return rating > 10 ? megaStars : stars;
8   }
9
10  export function TweetButton(props) {
11    const tweetURL = `https://twitter.com/intent/tweet?text=Thank+you,+%40oluwa
      ↪  tobiss.+Your+book+helped+me+create,+test,+and+publish+${
12      props.number && props.number > 1 ? props.number : "an"
13    }+NPM+${
14      props.number && props.number > 1 ? "packages" : "package"
15    }.%0A%0AMy+Favorite:+${props.bestNPMPackage}%0A%0ABook's+Rating:+${
16      props.rating
17    }-star+rating!+${generateStarIcons(
18      props.rating
19    )}+%0A%0ACreating%20NPM%20Package%0A%0Ahttps%3A%2F%2Famzn.to/4lifL3n`;
20
21    return props.rating && props.bestNPMPackage ? (
22      <section className="tweet-btn-container">
23        <a className="tweet-button" href={tweetURL} target="_blank">
24          Post a thank you tweet
25        </a>
26      </section>
27    ) : (
28      <div
29        style={{
30          display: "flex",
31          justifyContent: "center",
32          marginTop: "30px",
33        }}
34      >
35        <p
36          style={{
37            backgroundColor: "#DC3545",
38            color: "#fff",
39            width: "35%",
40            borderRadius: "5px",
41            padding: "15px 20px",
42          }}
43        >
44          Error: One or more required props are missing in 'TweetButtonProps'.
45        </p>
46      </div>
47    );
```

48   }

Run the build step:

Figure 156. Command Line

```
1   npm run build
```

 Test your updated package locally before you commit your changes. If you need to review the steps, see Chapter 10: Local Testing of Unpublished Package on page 45.

When ready to save your changes, run a commit as follows:

Figure 157. Command Line

```
1   git add -A && git commit -m "refactor(tweetbutton): change send text to post"
```

Then, push your commits to the remote repository to release the latest version.

Figure 158. Command Line

```
1   git push -u origin main
```

 This is a good time to test your latest release with your NextJS demo website. Make sure to update the test-app to the current version before running your tests. For example, run `npm install thank-you-tweet-button-001@latest`.

If you go to your project's GitHub repository and look at the "Releases" section, you will see only the project's tags, not its releases.

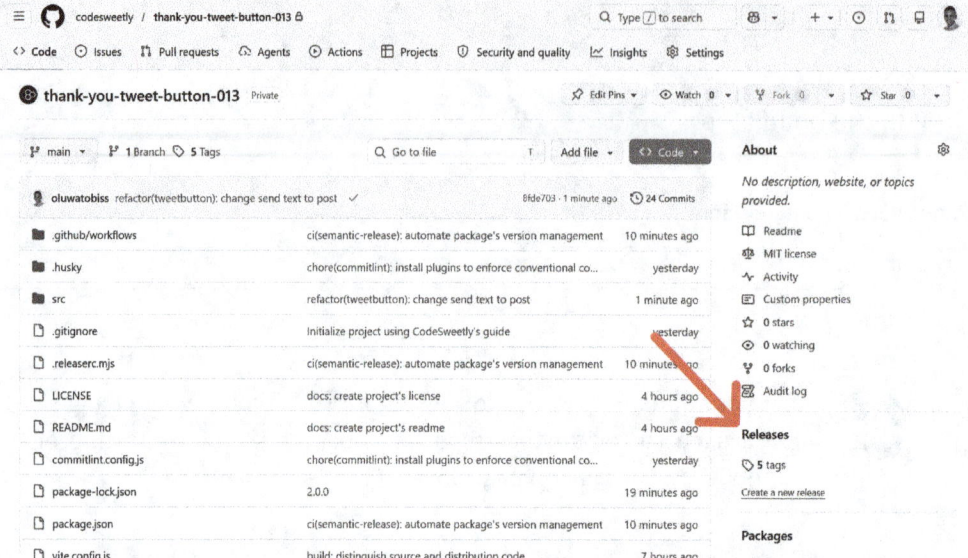

Figure 159. Red arrow pointing to the package's Releases section on GitHub

There are no releases yet because none have been published. In the next chapter, you will set up an automated process to fix this.

Automating GitHub Releases

The `semantic-release` library can be configured to automatically publish a package's release notes during a new version release. This process requires two primary steps:

1. Add the preset library to your release workflow.
2. Configure `semantic-release` to publish the release note.

Add the Preset Library to Your Release Workflow

Open your `release.yml` file and add the preset library needed to customize the release note to the workflow's install list:

Figure 160. release.yml: Add conventional-changelog-conventionalcommits library (line 33)

```
1  name: Release
2
3  on:
4    push:
5      branches:
6        - main
7
8  permissions:
9    id-token: write
10   contents: write
11
12  jobs:
13    release:
14      name: Semantic Release
15      runs-on: ubuntu-latest
16      steps:
17        - name: Checkout repository
18          uses: actions/checkout@v6
19          with:
20            fetch-depth: 0
21            persist-credentials: false
22
23        - name: Setup Node.js
```

```
24          uses: actions/setup-node@v6
25          with:
26            node-version: 24
27            registry-url: https://registry.npmjs.org
28
29        - name: Install semantic-release
30          run: |
31            npm install --no-save \
32              semantic-release@25 \
33              conventional-changelog-conventionalcommits@9 \
34
35        - name: Build package
36          run: npm run build
37
38        - name: Run semantic-release
39          env:
40            GITHUB_TOKEN: ${{ secrets.GITHUB_TOKEN }}
41          run: npx semantic-release
```

- `conventional-changelog-conventionalcommits`: a set of rules (pre-set) that `semantic-release` will use to format the release note.

Now, configure `semantic-release` to publish the release notes to GitHub.

Configure semantic-release to Automatically Publish the Package's Release Notes

To automatically create GitHub releases[1] for your project, add the `@semantic-release/github` plugin to your `.releaserc.mjs` file.

---
[1]https://docs.github.com/en/repositories/releasing-projects-on-github/about-releases

Figure 161. .releaserc.mjs: Set up semantic-release to publish release notes to GitHub (line 29-49, 51-58)

```
1   /**
2    * @type {import('semantic-release').GlobalConfig}
3    */
4   export default {
5     branches: ["main"],
6     repositoryUrl: "https://github.com/your-username/package-repo-name",
7     plugins: [
8       [
9         "@semantic-release/commit-analyzer",
10        {
11          preset: "conventionalcommits",
12          parserOpts: {
13            noteKeywords: ["BREAKING CHANGE", "BREAKING CHANGES"],
14          },
15          releaseRules: [
16            { breaking: true, release: "major" },
17            { type: "feat", release: "minor" },
18            { type: "fix", release: "patch" },
19            { type: "perf", release: "patch" },
20            { type: "refactor", release: "patch" },
21            { type: "docs", release: "patch" },
22            { type: "style", release: "patch" },
23            { type: "test", release: false },
24            { type: "chore", release: false },
25            { type: "ci", release: false },
26          ],
27        },
28      ],
29      [
30        "@semantic-release/release-notes-generator",
31        {
32          preset: "conventionalcommits",
33          presetConfig: {
34            types: [
35              { type: "feat", section: "Features" },
36              { type: "fix", section: "Bug Fixes" },
37              { type: "perf", section: "Performance" },
38              { type: "refactor", section: "Refactoring" },
39              { type: "docs", section: "Documentation" },
40              { type: "style", section: "Code Style" },
41            ],
42          },
43          writerOpts: {
44            groupBy: "type",
45            commitGroupsSort: "title",
46            commitsSort: ["scope", "subject"],
47          },
48        },
```

```
49        ],
50        ["@semantic-release/npm", { npmPublish: true }],
51        [
52          "@semantic-release/github",
53          {
54            successComment: false,
55            failComment: false,
56            releasedLabels: false,
57          },
58        ],
59      ],
60    };
```

- List @semantic-release/github as the last plugin in your setup. This way, the release announcement happens only after your package is built, committed, and published.
- Setting the successComment, failComment, and releasedLabels options to false prevents @semantic-release/github from commenting on or labeling issues and PRs. This also eliminates the need to grant the auto-generated GITHUB_TOKEN the issues: write and pull-requests: write permissions.

After you set up the release note's formatting and publication, stage and commit your changes using the Conventional Commits format.

Figure 162. Command Line

```
1  git add -A && git commit -m "ci: configure semantic-release to auto-publish
   ↪  project's github releases"
```

Also, change the button's text from "tweet" to "message".

Figure 163. TweetButton.jsx: Update line 24

```
1   function generateStarIcons(rating) {
2     const megaStars = `⭐⭐⭐⭐⭐ x ${Math.round(rating / 5)}`;
3     let stars = "";
4     for (let i = 0; i < rating; i++) {
5       stars += "⭐";
6     }
7     return rating > 10 ? megaStars : stars;
8   }
9
10  export function TweetButton(props) {
11    const tweetURL = `https://twitter.com/intent/tweet?text=Thank+you,+%40oluwa
      ↪   tobiss.+Your+book+helped+me+create,+test,+and+publish+${
12      props.number && props.number > 1 ? props.number : "an"
13    }+NPM+${
14      props.number && props.number > 1 ? "packages" : "package"
15    }.%0A%0AMy+Favorite:+${props.bestNPMPackage}%0A%0ABook's+Rating:+${
16      props.rating
17    }-star+rating!+${generateStarIcons(
18      props.rating
19    )}+%0A%0ACreating%20NPM%20Package%0A%0Ahttps%3A%2F%2Famzn.to/4lifL3n`;
20
21    return props.rating && props.bestNPMPackage ? (
22      <section className="tweet-btn-container">
23        <a className="tweet-button" href={tweetURL} target="_blank">
24          Post a thank you message
25        </a>
26      </section>
27    ) : (
28      <div
29        style={{
30          display: "flex",
31          justifyContent: "center",
32          marginTop: "30px",
33        }}
34      >
35        <p
36          style={{
37            backgroundColor: "#DC3545",
38            color: "#fff",
39            width: "35%",
40            borderRadius: "5px",
41            padding: "15px 20px",
42          }}
43        >
44          Error: One or more required props are missing in 'TweetButtonProps'.
45        </p>
46      </div>
47    );
```

48   }

Then, run the build step:

Figure 164. Command Line

1   npm run build

Test your updated package on your local machine before committing. If you need a refresher, see Chapter 10: Local Testing of Unpublished Package on page 45 for the steps.

When you are ready to save your changes, commit them as follows:

Figure 165. Command Line

1   git add -A && git commit -m "refactor(tweetbutton): change tweet text to
↪   message"

Next, push your commits to the remote repository to release the latest version of your project:

Figure 166. Command Line

1   git push -u origin main

Now, if you look at the "Releases" section on your GitHub repo's main page, you'll see your latest release.

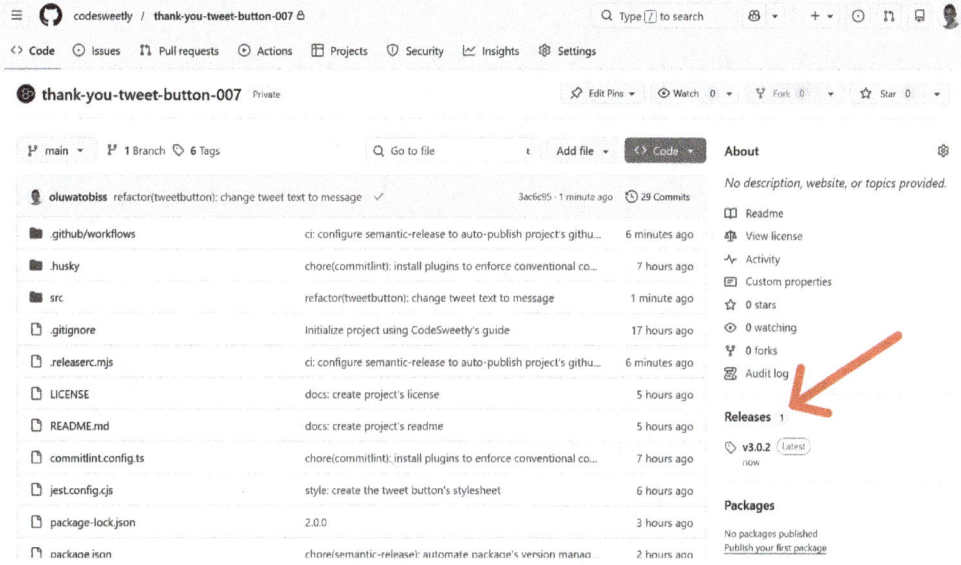

Figure 167. Red arrow showing the package's latest GitHub release

Click the latest release's label to see its notes and links to the binary files.

 This is a good time to test your latest release with your Nex-tJS demo site. Make sure to update the test app to the latest version before testing. For example, run `npm install thank-you-tweet-button-001@latest`.

Modular programming makes your codebase easier to manage. In the next chapter, you will see how to use this method in your React.js NPM Package Publishing project.

Modularizing JavaScript Codebase

Code modularization means breaking your codebase into separate files called modules[1]. Each module is an independent element that can be used in other parts of your project. This makes your code easier to read, maintain, and reuse. Here are the steps to modularize the TweetButton.jsx script.

1. Identify Independent Elements

Begin by identifying independent elements in the codebase suitable for extraction. For instance, TweetButton.jsx includes two such items: generateStarIcons and TweetButton.

Figure 168. TweetButton.jsx

```
1  function generateStarIcons(rating) {
2    const megaStars = `⭐⭐⭐⭐⭐ x ${Math.round(rating / 5)}`;
3    let stars = "";
4    for (let i = 0; i < rating; i++) {
5      stars += "⭐";
6    }
7    return rating > 10 ? megaStars : stars;
8  }
9
10 export function TweetButton(props) {
11   const tweetURL = `https://twitter.com/intent/tweet?text=Thank+you,+%40oluwa
     ↪   tobiss.+Your+book+helped+me+create,+test,+and+publish+${
12     props.number && props.number > 1 ? props.number : "an"
13   }+NPM+${
14     props.number && props.number > 1 ? "packages" : "package"
15   }.%0A%0AMy+Favorite:+${props.bestNPMPackage}%0A%0ABook's+Rating:+${
16     props.rating
17   }-star+rating!+${generateStarIcons(
18     props.rating
19   )}+%0A%0ACreating%20NPM%20Package%0A%0Ahttps%3A%2F%2Famzn.to/4lifL3n`;
20
21   return props.rating && props.bestNPMPackage ? (
22     <section className="tweet-btn-container">
```

---

[1]https://codesweetly.com/javascript-modules-tutorial

```
23        <a className="tweet-button" href={tweetURL} target="_blank">
24          Post a thank you message
25        </a>
26      </section>
27    ) : (
28      <div
29        style={{
30          display: "flex",
31          justifyContent: "center",
32          marginTop: "30px",
33        }}
34      >
35        <p
36          style={{
37            backgroundColor: "#DC3545",
38            color: "#fff",
39            width: "35%",
40            borderRadius: "5px",
41            padding: "15px 20px",
42          }}
43        >
44          Error: One or more required props are missing in 'TweetButtonProps'.
45        </p>
46      </div>
47    );
48  }
```

2. Split the Elements You Want to Extract into Their Separate Modules

Once you've identified the independent parts, create a new file for each item you want to separate. For example, `generateStarIcons` should each be placed in its own file.

Figure 169. Command Line

```
1  touch src/generateStarIcons.js
```

Next, transfer the relevant code from `TweetButton.jsx` into the new module file.

Assign each module a single responsibility in accordance with the single-responsibility principle[2]. This practice enhances readability, testability, and maintainability. Ensure that each module has all the code it needs.

Figure 170. generateStarIcons.js

```
1  export function generateStarIcons(rating) {
2    const megaStars = `★★★★★ x ${Math.round(rating / 5)}`;
3    let stars = "";
4    for (let i = 0; i < rating; i++) {
5      stars += "★";
6    }
7    return rating > 10 ? megaStars : stars;
8  }
```

- We use named exports for the generateStarIcons function because default exports can cause errors[3]. It's better for package authors to use named exports[4].
- Learn about default export[5].

3. Import the Extracted Elements into the TweetButton.jsx File

Import the generateStarIcons module into TweetButton.jsx and use it as shown below:

---

[2]https://en.wikipedia.org/wiki/Single-responsibility_principle
[3]https://esbuild.github.io/content-types/#default-interop
[4]https://codesweetly.com/javascript-modules-tutorial#how-to-export-a-modules-code
[5]https://codesweetly.com/javascript-modules-tutorial#how-to-export-anonymously-to-an-es-module

Figure 171. TweetButton.tsx: Import the generateStarIcons modules (line 1)

```
1   import { generateStarIcons } from "../generateStarIcons.js";
2
3   export function TweetButton(props) {
4     const tweetURL =
      ↪    `https://twitter.com/intent/tweet?text=Thank+you,+%40oluwatobiss.+Your+
5   book+helped+me+create,+test,+and+publish+${
6       props.number && props.number > 1 ? props.number : "an"
7   }+NPM+${
8       props.number && props.number > 1 ? "packages" : "package"
9   }.%0A%0AMy+Favorite:+${props.bestNPMPackage}%0A%0ABook's+Rating:+${
10      props.rating
11  }-star+rating!+${generateStarIcons(
12      props.rating
13  )}+%0A%0ACreating%20NPM%20Package%0A%0Ahttps%3A%2F%2Famzn.to/4lifL3n`;
14
15    return props.rating && props.bestNPMPackage ? (
16      <section className="tweet-btn-container">
17        <a className="tweet-button" href={tweetURL} target="_blank">
18          Post a thank you message
19        </a>
20      </section>
21    ) : (
22      <div
23        style={{
24          display: "flex",
25          justifyContent: "center",
26          marginTop: "30px",
27        }}
28      >
29        <p
30          style={{
31            backgroundColor: "#DC3545",
32            color: "#fff",
33            width: "35%",
34            borderRadius: "5px",
35            padding: "15px 20px",
36          }}
37        >
38          Error: One or more required props are missing in 'TweetButtonProps'.
39        </p>
40      </div>
41    );
42  }
```

Now, publish the latest version of your NPM package.

4. Release the Latest Version of the Project

First, run your tests to confirm everything works as expected:

Figure 172. Command Line

```
1  npm run test
```

Once all tests pass, run the build step:

Figure 173. Command Line

```
1  npm run build
```

 Test your updated package locally before committing your changes. If you need a reminder of the steps, see Chapter 10: Local Testing of Unpublished Package on page 45.

When ready to save your changes, run a commit:

Figure 174. Command Line

```
1  git add -A && git commit -m "refactor: modularize javascript code"
```

Next, push your commits to the remote repository to release the latest version of your project:

Figure 175. Command Line

```
1  git push -u origin main
```

 This is a good time to test your latest release with your NextJS demo site. Be sure to update the test app to the latest version before testing. For example, run npm install thank-you-tweet-button-001@latest.

Epilogue

Congratulations! You did it!

You're now an NPM package publisher. Whether automating workflows, managing versioning, or structuring your package like a pro, you've gained skills many developers take years to master through trial and error.

You now have what you need to build, test, and publish professional ReactJS libraries to NPM. That's no small accomplishment. You have taken a significant step toward becoming a more powerful, self-sufficient, and community-minded developer.

Here's how my project turned out:

- Package's GitHub Repo[1]
- Package's NPM Publication[2]

Now it's your turn to make an impact. Publish something great, share your work with others, and inspire people with what you create.

I'd love to see your library. Feel free to send me links[3] to your published work.

What's Next?

This isn't just the end of a book. It's the start of your journey as a confident NPM package author. The tools and best practices you've learned will save you time, streamline your projects, and help you share your code with the React community worldwide.

This is an ideal time to build upon the knowledge you have gained. Improvement comes with continued practice, so do not be discouraged if you still feel

---

[1]https://github.com/codesweetly/thank-you-tweet-button-002
[2]https://www.npmjs.com/package/thank-you-tweet-button-002
[3]mailto:oluwatobiss@codesweetly.com

uncertain about creating NPM packages. Consistent practice, development, and publication will lead to mastery.

Importantly, always take the bold step of deploying your libraries live for public use. You will be surprised by how much people will appreciate your product.

If you get stuck, come back to this guide to review the lessons. You can also explore the React TypeScript version of this book for even more advanced insights into publishing packages with added type safety.

One Last Favor

If you found this book helpful, I'd really appreciate it if you could leave a positive review where you bought it. Your feedback helps other developers find the book and helps us make it better for future readers.

Thank you for being part of the CodeSweetly learning community. Keep coding, keep creating, and keep shipping.

Happy packaging!

CodeSweetly[4]

---

[4]https://codesweetly.com

www.ingramcontent.com/pod-product-compliance
Lightning Source LLC
Chambersburg PA
CBHW081207290526
45796CB00009B/297